A Gift for :

_____

Presented by :

_____

Amen
to
That!

Amen to That!

{ **The Amazing Way the Bible Influences Our EVERYDAY LANGUAGE** }

Ferdie Addis

Reader's Digest

The Reader's Digest Association, Inc.
New York, NY • Montreal

A READER'S DIGEST BOOK

Copyright © 2014 Michael O'Mara Books Limited

First published in Great Britain in 2011 by Michael O'Mara Books Limited, 9 Lion Yard, Tremadoc Road, London SW4 7NQ

Library of Congress Cataloging-in-Publication Data

Addis, Ferdie, 1983-
  Amen to that! : the amazing way the bible influences our everyday language / Ferdie Addis.
      pages cm.
  Includes bibliographical references and index.
   Summary: "this fascinating, fun-to-read collection reveals hundreds of familiar centuries-old expressions that originated from the Bible--and the stories behind them. Many of us have never read or studied the Bible, yet people have been quoting from its pages for centuries, not knowing the origin or significance of these timeless expressions. Let there be light! Amen to That will delightfully shed clarity on how a collection of ancient stories, written in three languages over the course of a thousand years, has had such an impact on the way we speak today"-- Provided by publisher.
   ISBN 978-1-62145-107-5 -- ISBN 978-1-62145-108-2 (epub)
   1. Bible--Miscellanea. 2. English language--Terms and phrases--History.
I. Title.
  BS615.A33 2013
  220--dc23

                                    2013014462

We are committed to both the quality of our products and the service we provide to our customers. We value your comments, so please feel free to contact us.

          The Reader's Digest Association, Inc.
          Adult Trade Publishing
          44 South Broadway
          White Plains, NY 10601

For more Reader's Digest products and information, visit our website:
          www.rd.com (in the United States)
          www.readersdigest.ca (in Canada)

Printed in the United States of America

1 3 5 7 9 10 8 6 4 2

Acknowledgments

Many thanks to Kate Moore, who knew what she wanted from this book and helped me to achieve it; to Ana Bjezancevic for her beautiful cover and Graeme Andrew for the design; to Reverend Dr. Peter Mullen for kindly reading the text; and to Laura Palmer, who makes everything possible.

Introduction

No book in history has contributed more phrases to the English language than the King James Bible. Published in 1611, after years of toil by a crack team of biblical scholars, this "labor of love" has been "weighed in the balance" for centuries and has never "fallen from grace." It is read even at "the ends of the earth." It "breathes life" into our everyday language and helps us "see eye to eye." It has "put words into our mouths" and has been "all things to all men."

These days, biblical sayings come up in everything from sports (a Hail Mary pass) to Westerns (Jumpin' Jehosephat) to video games ("an eye for an eye" is a magic spell in an online RPG).

Sometimes we refer to Bible stories more deliberately. We praise "good Samaritans" and avoid "doubting Thomases." With "the wisdom of Solomon" we dodge the "serpent in every paradise" and "wash our hands" of those who bear "the mark of Cain."

We steal proverbs and snippets of advice from the Bible too, telling each other to "turn the other cheek" and to "do as you would be done by." We "let not the sun go down on our wrath" and we "reap what we sow."

Then there are moments when the grand language of the King James comes in useful for rhetorical effect. "How are the mighty fallen," we say with a verbal flourish. "No rest for the wicked," we complain wryly. And when good things do come our way, we greet them fulsomely with a "Hallelujah" or an "Amen to that."

So how did a collection of ancient stories, written in three languages over the course of a thousand years, have such an impact on the way we speak today?

You might say the answer's obvious. The Bible is a holy book for three of humanity's great religions. Billions of believers around the world regard it as the sacred word of God.

But the story is more complicated than that. After all, the Bible wasn't even translated into English until the 1380s, and the project was so controversial that its leader, John Wycliffe, was declared a heretic by the Roman Catholic Church. After Wycliffe's death, the Pope ordered that his body be dug up and burned to ashes, to cleanse the world of his shocking blasphemy.

The next great translator was William Tyndale, the genius of the English Reformation, whose version had a huge influence on later editions. The poetry of his words was unsurpassed but his Bible was brutally suppressed, and he himself was strangled and burned at the stake in 1536.

Finally, at the beginning of the seventeenth century, the King James Bible makes its first triumphant appearance. Commissioned by James I to be the definitive English translation of the Good Book, it was produced in three different cities by a committee of fifty-four scholars with representatives from all the squabbling branches of Anglo-Saxon Protestantism. Their task was to somehow create a Bible that would be acceptable to everyone from High Church Anglicans to the fiery Covenanters of the Scottish Borders.

It sounds like a recipe for disaster. But by some strange accident of fate or providence, this many-headed team produced a beautiful and poetic text to rival any work of English literature before or since.

The style was noble and archaic to evoke the greatness of the Lord of Hosts. The language, simple and muscular, was designed for the ear of the common man. This was not a Bible for the clerical elite, but one for the people. Soon, copies could be found in churches all over Britain, and the ringing words of the King James Bible were heard by illiterate peasants and well-bred lords alike.

It was a seminal moment in the evolution of English language and literature. This single book became a universal cultural reference point; a shared foundation for later poets and thinkers. Coleridge claimed that studying the King James would keep any writer from becoming "vulgar, in point of style." Winston Churchill called it a "masterpiece." Writers as diverse as Milton, Swift and Scott have borrowed liberally from its pages.

You don't have to be a Christian to appreciate its significance. Even the scientist Richard Dawkins, famous for his militant atheism, confessed to a "lifelong love" for the King James translation, and called it a "precious heritage." Christopher Hitchens, another confirmed secularist, admired its "crystalline prose."

But it was Andrew Motion, a former British Poet Laureate, who best captured the depth, scope and importance of the King James Bible. To read it, he said, "is to feel simultaneously at home, a citizen of the world and a traveller through eternity."

Ferdie Addis

Adam's Apple

[Genesis 3:3–6]

A prominent lump that appears on men's throats as they reach puberty

The Adam's apple is a colloquial name for the small bump over a man's larynx. It's caused by the stretching of the thyroid cartilage as the voice breaks during puberty and is just one of many so-called "secondary sexual characteristics," no more important than facial hair or large feet.

That hasn't, of course, stopped humans from investing this stray lump of gristle with the usual dose of symbolic significance. As early as 1755, the first ever English dictionary (by Samuel Johnson) records the use of "Adam's Apple" to describe this modest part, based on the belief that part of the forbidden fruit got stuck in Adam's throat when he ate it in the Garden of Eden. Eve's bite of apple, by contrast, slipped down without a hitch—exactly what eighteenth-century Englishmen would have expected from the "weaker sex."

These days, the Adam's apple most often appears in pop culture as a telltale mark of male-to-female transvestites. Internet humorists have even coined the term "Madam's apple" to describe a suspicious laryngeal lump appearing on an otherwise alluring woman.

Amen to That

[Deuteronomy 27:27; Matthew 6:13]

A strong statement of agreement

In the earliest Bible translations, the word "amen" doesn't feature at all. Like any other Hebrew word it gets translated—to "so it is," or in Old English *Sóðlice*. By the 1382 Wycliffe edition, "amen" had begun to be used as an English word, for example at the end of the Lord's Prayer in Matthew's Gospel.

Amen became a standard ending to all prayers, indicating a general assent to whatever has been said before. In 1605, the phrase "amen to that" was first used in a non-religious sense in an anonymous drama called *King Leir* (not to be confused with Shakespeare's *King Lear*). Charles Dickens picks it up in the *Pickwick Papers,* as does Agatha Christie a hundred years later in *The Mysterious Affair at Styles*: " 'We do hope, if there has been foul play, to bring the murderer to justice.' 'Amen to that,' said Dorcas fiercely."

"Amen" also gives us the old American expression "Amen corner," meaning a group of fervent believers. It comes from the practice of sitting the most vocally pious people near the pulpit in Methodist churches, from where they could lead the communal "amens."

An Apocryphal Story

[Deuteronomy 27:27; Matthew 6:13]

A story that is spurious or untrue, although often appealing

The Bible is generally imagined as a single coherent tome, handed down through generations—perhaps from God himself. In fact, it's more like an anthology. Bits of ancient lore from all sorts of different sources were gathered together, over years, and arranged into the familiar patchwork of books we know today.

What's more, some texts failed to make the grade. The earliest Bibles have several extra books—from the mythological fantasies of Enoch to the worldly proverbs of the Wisdom of Sirach—that were cut from later editions, as doubts emerged as to whether they were the authentic word of God.

These books are collectively known as the "apocrypha," from the Greek *apokryphos*, meaning "secret" or "hidden," and although they contain fascinating (and highly respected) stories they are generally regarded as having been created long after the traditional books of the Old Testament.

The opposite of "apocryphal" has also become a common word in modern English, especially among fans of video games, comic books and other fantasy franchises. When some new addition to a series appears—like a new *Star Wars* game, for example—Web forums often come alive with heated debate about whether or not the latest fiction is strictly "canonical," a word that comes from the idea of the biblical "canon."

The Apple of My Eye

[Deuteronomy 32:10; Psalms 7:8]

A precious or much-loved person or thing

These days we are used to thinking of the eye as a sort of white ball filled with clear jelly. The pupil is like an aperture on a camera—a black hole that lets light in to form its inverted image on the hidden retina.

To medieval scientists, however, this model of the eye would have seemed entirely back to front. The pupil, they believed, was a solid round black ball, from which the eye shone invisible "eye-beams" to build a picture of the world outside. So when King Alfred in the ninth century was translating the Latin *pupillae* into Old English, he called them the æpplas of the *eagum*—the "apples" of the "eye."

The use of the pupil of the eye as a metaphor for something dear or precious goes back far beyond King Alfred though. The Book of Deuteronomy uses the phrase to describe God's relationship to the Hebrew Patriarch Jacob. Of course, the original Hebrew (later translated as *pupilla* and then "apple") makes no mention of Alfred's ocular fruit. In fact, it literally means something like "the little man of the eye"—a possible reference to the way people who look closely at each other's eyes can see themselves there as tiny reflections.

Après Moi le Déluge

[Genesis 7–8]

Literally "After me, the flood'

This odd expression is attributed to Madame de Pompadour, the famous lover of King Louis XV of France. After a combined French-Austrian army was defeated by the Germans at the battle of Rossbach in 1757, she made the remark to her royal paramour, anticipating a catastrophe on the scale of the Deluge (better known as Noah's Flood).

It was a prophetic statement. After Louis XV's death, his successor proved incapable of running the country, which soon erupted in the bloody convulsions of the French Revolution.

A few decades later, the Austrian statesman Metternich repeated the saying. His meaning was that without his influence the established order in Austria would collapse, and the phrase is still used today to describe the veiled threats of autocrats who present themselves as critical to international stability, a tactic that was used repeatedly by the tottering dictators of the so-called "Arab Spring."

But although the Deluge may be something to be afraid of, you can't hold it off forever without stagnation. After all, whenever an idea or attitude is considered particularly primitive or old-fashioned, critics will sneer that it's "antediluvian"—literally, "from before the flood."

No Balm in Gilead

[Jeremiah 8:22]

No consolation or hope

This unusual phrase comes from the Book of Jeremiah. The prophet laments the suffering of Israel saying: "Is there no balm in Gilead? Is there no physician there?"

"Balm" is the resin of *Balsamodendron* trees—a well-known medicine in the ancient world and one for which the region of Gilead (in modern Jordan) was famous. For Gilead to run out of balm is, in the Bible, a powerful sign that Israel is in dire straits.

African slaves brought to America in the eighteenth and nineteenth centuries famously answered Jeremiah's question in a traditional spiritual called, in a remarkable display of optimism, "There is a balm in Gilead."

These days, "Gilead" usually crops up as a literary reference (for example, as the name of a future American dystopia in Margaret Atwood's 1985 novel *The Handmaid's Tale*). "Balm," used on its own, is more common, in phrases like "a balm for the soul."

A Baptism of Fire

[Matthew 3:11]

A painful ordeal; a difficult introduction to something

In nineteenth-century Europe, soldiers would speak proudly of their "baptisms of fire"—the first time they ever faced enemy bullets. This was regarded as an important rite of passage. Indeed, the fourteen-year-old French Prince Louis Napoleon deliberately, and with his father's permission, exposed himself to enemy shots at the battle of Saarbrücken in 1870 in order to get his baptism of fire done with early.

That nineteenth-century ritual is what leads to the common modern meaning of the phrase. Originally, however, the "baptism of fire" was not a physical ordeal but rather a spiritual blessing. In Matthew's Gospel, John the Baptist tells a crowd: "I indeed baptize you with water unto repentance: but he that cometh after me is mightier than I . . . He shall baptize you with the Holy Ghost, and with fire."

The expression is still used in theological contexts to describe the spiritual aspect of baptism, as opposed to the physical action performed by a priest. It can also be applied to those Christian martyrs for whom a "baptism of fire" meant being burned at the stake.

Be All Things to All Men

[1 Corinthians 9:22]

To try to please everyone by appearing similar to them

In St. Paul's First Letter to the Corinthians, he explains his tactics as an apostle. He has, he says, made himself "a servant unto all"—preaching to Jews, he acts "as a Jew"; among the weak, he acts like someone who is weak; "to them that are without law, as without law." So, he tells his readers, "I am made all things to all men, that I might by all means save some."

The approach clearly worked—no one could doubt St. Paul's success at spreading Christianity—but in modern English the phrase has come to describe a negative approach. It's an accusation often hurled at politicians, for example, that they try to be all things to all men and so have no real substance of their own. In the words of another popular proverb: "You can't please everyone."

The Beam in Your Own Eye

[Matthew 7:3–5]

Your own failings, as opposed to someone else's; used to accuse someone of hypocrisy

The parable of the mote and the beam comes from the Sermon on the Mount, in Matthew's Gospel. Jesus tells the story of a man who points out a splinter in his friend's eye while, rather implausibly, failing to notice the great log that is sitting in his own. After all, Jesus points out, if you're going to perform some impromptu ocular surgery on someone, it's better to do it when you're not blinded yourself by a giant plank of wood.

As a way of pointing out the failings of critics, the allusion has been popular in English since at least 1377, when

William Langland used it in his poem *Piers Plowman* (B x.264). More recently, the phrase has been a favorite with opinionated journalists, accusing the world's do-gooders of hypocrisy. Oddly though, and if anything this proves Jesus' point, the beam is always in someone else's eye, never in their own.

Bear the Mark of Cain

[Genesis 4:1–15]

Be marked as a murderer; to be guilty

After Cain murders his brother Abel in the Book of Genesis, God condemns him to wander the Earth, cursed forever to be an outcast. To sweeten the pill, God puts a mysterious mark on the unhappy fratricide to ensure that no one he meets will go as far as actually killing him.

In modern usage, however, the mark of Cain is not thought of as a mercy, but as a spiritual stain of guilt that attaches to murderers. The phrase is fairly unusual today, but it got a huge boost in popularity when Colonel Tim Collins used it in a speech on the eve of the Iraq War. "Men who have taken life needlessly," he warned his troops, "live with the mark of Cain upon them." This strict warning was the inspiration for a 2007 television film about soldiers in Iraq, which took "the mark of Cain" for its title.

But some have taken the mark of Cain more literally. Controversy still surrounds the writings of the founders of the Mormon Church in the early nineteenth century, who appear to have interpreted the mark to mean black skin. African slaves, therefore, were considered to be the descendants of Cain, still rightfully laboring under God's curse.

Cain and Abel

Cain and Abel were the first sons of Adam and Eve after they were expelled from the Garden of Eden. Cain, the older, was an agriculturalist, and offered the "fruit of the ground" as a sacrifice to God. Abel, the pastoralist, went one better, tempting the Lord with a succulent array of freshly barbecued lambs.

God rejects Cain's vegetarian platter but accepts Abel's roast with enthusiasm. Cain, in a jealous fury, kills his brother in a field. When God inquires as to Abel's whereabouts, Cain famously and rudely replies: "Am I my brother's keeper?"

As one might expect, God is not taken in by this surly protest of ignorance and Cain is condemned to wander the earth as an outcast the rest of his life. In the Middle Ages it was sometimes said that Cain was still wandering and would continue his lonely exile until the end of the world.

To Beard the Lion

[1 Samuel 17:34]

Confront someone aggressively, especially on his own turf

The First Book of Samuel tells how David, then just a shepherd boy, convinces King Saul that he should be allowed to fight the Philistine champion Goliath. "Thy servant," he says, "kept his father's sheep, and there came a lion, and a bear, and took a lamb out of the flock."

David, of course, took this unusual example of animal cooperation in his stride: "I went out after him, and smote him . . . and when he arose against me, I caught him by his beard, and smote him, and slew him."

With all the smiting, grabbing the lion's beard (lions do in fact have a patch of tufty hair under the chin) might seem a bit unnecessary. But for ancient Israelites, as with many other Middle Eastern cultures, a man's beard was a symbol of his dignity and virility. To touch or grasp someone's beard was to offer the ultimate insult.

Walter Scott, in his 1808 epic poem *Marmion*, gave this phrase the final poetic flourish, cementing its modern form in the English language:

> And darest thou then
> To beard the lion in his den,
> The Douglas in his hall?
> (xiv.23-5)

To Beat Swords into Plowshares

[Isaiah 2:4]

To turn from war to peace

In the "last days," says the Book of Isaiah, the people of the world "shall beat their swords into plowshares, and their spears into pruning hooks: nation shall not lift up sword against nation, neither shall they learn war any more."

This is a less fanciful image than it sounds. In the ancient world, metal was a scarce and precious commodity. The ancient Israelites were mostly farmers, and when they needed to defend their land, they were often forced to improvise weapons out of agricultural tools. A pruning hook—essentially a curved blade on a long pole—could easily be straightened into a spear, and a simple sword could be forged from the cutting blade of a primitive plough.

Although the phrase is now relatively rare, the basic idea remains a powerful one. Even today, at least one charity in Africa is trying to do exactly as Isaiah suggested, forging hoes and other tools out of melted-down AK-47s.

A Behemoth

[Job 40:15–24]

A huge animal; anything extremely large

The behemoth is a mysterious animal mentioned in the Book of Job. With bones "like bars of iron" and a tail "like a cedar," this mighty beast was said to be able to suck the whole River Jordan into its mouth. Biblical scholars have long debated whether the behemoth is a mythical creature or just an exaggerated description of an ordinary animal (the most popular candidate is a hippopotamus).

But whatever the original "behemoth" may have been, the name has become a metaphor for anything that reaches spectacular size. This figurative use is first recorded in a pamphlet of 1593, written by Gabriel Harvey as part of his vicious literary feud with Thomas Nashe. Nashe, writes Harvey, is "a Behemoth of conceit," but "a shrimp in wit, a periwinkle in art, a dandiprat in industry," and "a dodkin in value."

It's Better to Give Than to Receive

[Acts 20:35]

Giving is better than getting

This generous proverb comes from the Book of Acts, which describes the doings of the apostles after the death of Jesus. St. Paul, gathering the elders of the Church of Ephesus (a prosperous Greek city on the coast of what is now Turkey), tells them: "Remember the words of the Lord Jesus, how he said, 'It is more blessed to give than to receive.'"

Oddly, although Paul presents this as a direct quotation, careful examination of the Gospels reveals no record that Jesus ever said any such thing. But even if Jesus never said it, the old adage turns out to be verifiably true. A paper published in the journal *Science* in 2008 by researchers at Harvard Business School revealed that giving money away is directly correlated with happiness.

Bite the Dust

[Psalm 72:9; Micah 7:17; Genesis 3:19; Job 21:26]

To die; to fail

In the Bible, dust means death. "Unto dust shalt thou return," says God to Adam when he cuts him off from the Garden of Eden and the Tree of Life. "They shall lie down alike in the dust, and the worms shall cover them," says the Book of Job.

Although "bite the dust" sounds biblical, and is often listed as a Bible phrase, the closest the Bible comes to that precise wording is "lick the dust," which appears in Psalms and Micah as an expression of abasement and humiliation.

Licking doesn't turn into biting until as late as 1750, and the saying only takes off when it becomes a favorite cowboy catchphrase in the Wild West adventure stories of the nineteenth century. From there, it was adopted by RAF pilots in the Second World War (with their short life expectancies, they needed a lot of euphemisms for "to die").

The real high point for the expression comes in 1980, when a track called "Another One Bites the Dust" became a massive hit for glam-rock megastars Queen. Not that the song had much to do with death—in fact, some especially attentive listeners claimed the record's real message could only be heard if you played it backwards: "It's fun to smoke marijuana."

The Blind Leading the Blind

A situation where leaders don't know any better than those who follow them

This common expression comes from an unusual moment in the Bible when Jesus shows his sterner side by roundly criticizing a gang of irritating Pharisees. First he calls them "hypocrites" and then, when the shocked disciples warn him that the Pharisees are getting offended, he effectively says they should get stuffed: "Let them alone! They be blind leaders of the blind. And if the blind lead the blind, both shall fall into the ditch."

The phrase quickly became proverbial, given extra fame by a 1568 painting by Pieter Bruegel the Elder, which shows a troop of blind men pratfalling desperately into the mud with great comic aplomb. In modern usage, the warning about the ditch is generally left out—"the blind leading the blind" has become a useful shorthand description for any case of failing leadership, especially popular among disgruntled opinion writers whose distaste for politicians is exceeded only by their disdain for the people who actually voted for them.

Incidentally, although the use of this phrase in English goes back only as far as the Bible, the saying itself was probably ancient even in Jesus' day. A similar proverb appears in the Hindu *Katha Upanishad*, written centuries earlier.

Breathe Life into Something

....

[Genesis 2:7]

To inspire, or animate

These days, we tend to talk about "breathing life" in a very metaphorical way. You can breathe life into a dying idea, for example, or an unpopular government, even a dull party.

But in the Bible, the first "breath of life" was both very literal and hugely important. "The Lord God formed man of the dust of the ground," we are told in the Book of Genesis, "and breathed into his nostrils the breath of life; and man became a living soul."

This idea that breath was a kind of life force was widespread in ancient cultures. The Stoic philosophers of Greece and Rome used the word *pneuma* (breath) to describe the soul. The Presocratic writer Anaximenes went further, claiming that *pneuma* is the only element, from which the whole world is derived. Farther east, the Hindu Vedas taught that *prana* (breath) was the fundamental life force. In the same way, the Chinese *qi*, or spirit energy, can be literally translated as "breath" or "gas."

This idea has left its mark on our language in more ways than one. When a person receives a sudden flash of creativity or vitality, we say they are "inspired"—from the Latin *inspiro* (I breath into). A dead person, on the other hand, has "expired"—from *expiro* (I breathe out).

Cast Pearls Before Swine

[Matthew 7:6]

To waste something valuable on those who can't appreciate it

This famous phrase is a quote from Matthew's Gospel: "Give not that which is holy unto the dogs," writes the Evangelist, "neither cast ye your pearls before swine, lest they trample them under their feet, and turn again and rend you."

This dramatic image—which of course gains extra power from the fact that pigs are considered unclean animals by orthodox Jews—became a favorite in the Middle Ages, first mentioned in English by William Langland in *Piers Plowman* in the fourteenth century. Charles Dickens used the phrase in his 1848 novel *Dombey and Son*, to mean "doing a thankless thing."

But the most famous occurrence, which gives a twist to

the ancient meaning, is in a story about Dorothy Parker, the great American humorist of the 1920s. "Age before beauty," said a cheeky young woman while holding a door open for Parker to pass. Quick as a flash Parker replied: "Pearls before swine."

Cover a Multitude of Sins

[1 Peter 4:8]

Hide (often minor) defects

The First Epistle of Peter, supposedly written by the apostle himself around the end of the first century AD, offers the following advice to Christians of the Early Church: "Above all things have fervent charity among yourselves: for charity shall cover the multitude of sins."

The phrase has stuck in English, but in modern usage it has lost its serious intent. The sins that are covered tend to be of the trivial sort, and the thing that does the covering is as likely to be a flattering sweater as a divine virtue.

A Cross to Bear

[Matthew 10:38; Luke 14:27]

A personal trial or affliction

In the process of conquering half the known world, the ancient Romans became very adept at putting people to death. Mere injury, however savage, was not enough. Instead, ancient executions were arranged with a good solid dose of insult too—the public humiliation serving as a dreadful warning to other potential miscreants.

So when Jesus was condemned to die, the Gospels record, he was also forced to parade half naked through the streets of Jerusalem, carrying the cross to which he would later be nailed. His path through the city became known as the Via Dolorosa—the Way of Suffering—and is still marked in Jerusalem today.

But Jesus was not going to suffer alone. In a sermon from before his arrest, he tells his followers: "Whosoever doth not bear his cross, and come after me, cannot be my disciple."

The word "cross" has been used in English as a symbol for the trials and hardships of life since the sixteenth century. The first disciples, though, followed in Jesus' footsteps in a much more literal fashion. Of the original twelve apostles, only one, according to Christian tradition, died of natural causes. The others, except for Judas, were all martyred for their faith, with five of them actually crucified.

To Crucify

[Matthew 27:33; Mark 15:22; Luke 23:33; John 19:17]

To torment or destroy someone

The image of Jesus on the cross is one of the most powerful and familiar religious symbols in the world. In churches on every continent hang crucifixes of every description, from the ornate and elaborate to the simple and abstract. But as the symbol has become—thankfully—more familiar than the real thing, it's easy to forget that crucifixion really was an extremely unpleasant way to die.

Victims were whipped until they bled, then fixed to a cross, sometimes with rope but often with thick iron nails driven through the bones of the wrist and heel. In fact, the whole experience was so horrifyingly painful (the word "crucify" is from the same Latin root as "excruciating") that if they broke a prisoner's legs beforehand it was probably an act of mercy—at least it meant a quick death instead of hours and days at the mercy of the sun and of birds of prey.

More than that, crucifixion was a common form of execution, fit for slaves and murderers, not a unique punishment for the Son of God. After the famous slave revolt of 73 BC, the Romans had crucified fully six thousand rebels all at once, lining them up along a main road like grisly milestones. Jesus, meanwhile, shared Golgotha (the hill of the crucifixion) with a pair of thieves who hung by his side.

My Cup Runneth Over

I'm overwhelmed with good things

This famous Bible quote comes from Psalm 23, a famously beautiful song of praise traditionally attributed, like the other psalms, to King David himself. "Thou preparest a table before me in the presence of mine enemies," writes the lyrical monarch. "Thou anointest my head with oil; my cup runneth over." The psalm has been repeatedly set to music by composers as distinguished as J. S. Bach and Vaughan Williams and—rather incongruously given its cheery themes of plenty and happiness—is a major hit at funerals.

The phrase is widely used in modern English—sometimes to express gratitude and sometimes sarcastically, rather in the same manner as "gee, thanks!" Surprisingly, the image has also proved extremely popular with rappers and rock stars. Among the musical legends to have quoted David's Psalm are such noted Bible scholars as Eminem, Jay-Z, Alice in Chains, and even a Belgian death-metal band called Aborted.

A Damascene Conversion

[Acts 9:3–9]

**A sudden or inexplicable switch of opinion,
often from one extreme to another**

The Book of Acts describes how one Saul, a notorious persecutor of Christians, was travelling to Damascus to arrest some unfortunate believers. "Suddenly there shined round about him a light from heaven. And he fell to the earth, and heard a voice saying unto him, Saul, Saul, why persecutest thou me?"

This blast of the divine presence called for what you might call a severe re-evaluation of priorities. Thenceforth, Saul would be known as Paul, becoming the great evangelist and thinker of early Christianity. The former persecutor probably did more than any other man to define the shape of the embryonic Church.

In modern usage, though, a "damascene conversion" sometimes has negative overtones, suggesting that a change of heart has happened suspiciously quickly, and is often used of politicians and world leaders by the press.

A David and Goliath Contest

[1 Samuel 17]

A contest between unequally matched opponents

The First Book of Samuel, in the Old Testament, tells the story of a battle in the Valley of Elah, between a Philistine army on one side and an army of Israelites, led by King Saul, on the other. So far so conventional, but the Philistines stymie the Israelites by using a bold new tactic. From out of the Philistine lines comes a 9-foot-tall giant called Goliath, who dares the Israelite soldiers to face him in single combat.

Acceptance rates for this unappealing invitation are predictably low, and the Israelites' morale is sinking. Finally a young shepherd boy called David takes up Goliath's challenge, striding out, to general amazement, with no weapons but a stout staff and a leather slingshot.

Naturally Goliath is unimpressed, and promises to "give David's flesh to the birds of the air and the beasts of the field." But a more observant champion might have noticed a certain ominous glint of religious zeal in David's eye. With the unsettling confidence of the true believer, he replies, "This day the Lord will hand you over to me."

So it proves. While Goliath lumbers forward in his shining armor, David slings a pebble directly at the towering fighter, knocks him out cold, and proceeds to hack off the unfortunate man's head. The shepherd boy goes on to be Israel's greatest and most famous king.

In modern usage, all sorts of embattled minorities have taken inspiration from David's fight against Goliath. Unfortunately, in real life, it's Goliath who usually wins.

David and Jonathan

[1 Samuel 18:1–4; 2 Samuel 1:26]

Proverbial example of a close male friendship

The friendship between David and Jonathan is one of the Bible's most famous and interesting relationships. David, still a shepherd boy, kills Goliath and becomes a favorite of King Saul and his son, Jonathan. The First Book of Samuel tells how "the soul of Jonathan was knit with the soul of David, and Jonathan loved him as his own soul."

When Jonathan dies, years later, David is stricken. "I am distressed for thee, my brother Jonathan," he laments. "Very pleasant hast thou been unto me. Thy love to me was wonderful, passing the love of women."

Since then, Jonathan and David have been used as an archetype for any close male friendship. Presidents Teddy Roosevelt and William Taft, for example, were sarcastically compared to David and Jonathan by a Missouri senator in 1912.

Those august statesmen would doubtless have been shocked to learn that some scholars now regard the biblical friendship as a homosexual affair. This is, unsurprisingly, a controversial view. David was, after all, a married man (he paid the unusual dowry of two hundred Philistine foreskins to wed one of Saul's daughters).

But romantic friendships between men were hardly rare in the ancient world. The Greek hero Achilles had his Patroclus. Alexander the Great had Hephaestion. Julius Caesar was rumored to have lost his virginity to the King of Bithynia. An affair between David and Jonathan might seem unlikely, but it can't be ruled out.

A Disciple

....

[Matthew 4:19; Luke 14:26–33]

An ardent follower

The twelve disciples, from the Latin *discipulus*, meaning "student," were the closest followers of Jesus, who followed him on his preaching tour of the Holy Land. The most important was Simon "the Rock" Peter, who Jesus appointed as the first leader of the Christian Church.

The famous story, as told in Matthew's Gospel, is that Jesus found Simon Peter fishing on the shores of the Sea of Galilee with his brother. When he called them, the two abandoned their nets—a major sacrifice in days when nets had to be knotted by hand—and followed him, becoming, as the Bible oddly puts it, "fishers of men."

The number of the disciples, one for each of the twelve tribes of Israel, may be the source for one of the world's most enduring superstitions. At the Last Supper there were thirteen people sitting at the table. One was Jesus. Eleven were loyal disciples. The thirteenth was Judas Iscariot, the betrayer of Jesus, whose evil reputation has made 13 an unlucky number ever since.

Do As You Would Be Done By

[Luke 6:31]

**Act towards other people as you would
like them to act to you**

In Luke's Gospel, Jesus tells an assembled crowd: "As ye
would that men should do to you, do ye also to them like-
wise." This maxim would become one of the most famous
moral principles of all time.

The most familiar form today is "do as you would
be done by," which dates back to at least the seventeenth century, when it appeared in the journal of the
Quaker George Fox. Pithier than the original, it quickly
caught on. One Victorian novelist (C. Kingsley, *The
Water Babies*, 1863) even created a character called Mrs.
Doasyouwouldbedoneby, who he called "the loveliest
fairy in the world."

The thought expressed in the phrase, and others like it,
is known to philosophers as the "Golden Rule." Versions
of it can be found in ancient Egyptian papyri and in the
writings of Greek philosophers.

A Doubting Thomas

[John 20:24–29]

**A doubter; someone who refuses to believe
something without proof**

St. Thomas was one of the twelve disciples, but his brief moment of biblical fame doesn't arrive until after Jesus has been executed on the cross and buried in his tomb. Three days after the crucifixion, Jesus appears to the disciples and explains that he has risen from the dead and is on his way to heaven.

This is very comforting for everyone except Thomas who, for some reason, misses the all-important meeting. When his friends tell him the good news, he is skeptical. "Except I shall see in his hands the print of the nails," he says, "and thrust my hand into his side, I will not believe."

Thomas should have been careful what he wished for. Eight days later, Jesus appears to his doubting disciple, still dripping blood from his holy wounds. "Reach hither thy hand," he says, "and thrust it into my side and be not faithless, but believing."

Confronted with the physical (and gory) reality of the Messiah, Thomas becomes a believer—but Jesus is not impressed. His words have become a crucial statement of the importance of faith in Christian doctrine: "Because thou hast seen me, thou hast believed. Blessed are they that have not seen, and yet have believed."

A Drop in the Bucket

[Isaiah 40:15, 17]

Something negligible or insignificant

Stuck between the mighty pharaohs on one side, and a succession of great Mesopotamian empires on the other, Israel was always destined to be a small fish in a big and dangerous pond. By the middle of the sixth century BC, the Jewish kingdoms had been conquered repeatedly, and a decent chunk of the population was living in painful exile in Babylon.

Amid all this geopolitical gloom, the Book of Isaiah had some words of comfort. Compared to God, says the prophet, "the nations are as a drop of a bucket, and are counted as the small dust of the balance."

These days, in keeping with the modern enthusiasm for "super-sizing," the "bucket" is often replaced with the "ocean."

Eat, Drink and Be Merry

....

[Ecclesiastes 8:15; Isaiah 22:13]

Stop worrying and have a good time

Ecclesiastes is one of the Bible's odder books. Its author claims to be a son of the famous King David, and his work is essentially just a long series of maxims and aphorisms on the meaning of life. His conclusion? The actions of men on Earth don't really mean that much at all.

Luckily, his response to this problem is fairly cheerful: "Then I commended mirth," he writes, "because a man hath no better thing under the sun, than to eat, and to drink, and to be merry."

But it's not all fun and games. Later in the Bible, for instance in the Book of Isaiah, the same thought appears with a savage sting in the tail: "Let us eat and drink, for tomorrow we shall die."

The two quotes were popular in the nineteenth century, and gradually began to merge into a single phrase. By the 1880s, newspapers were happily misquoting: "Eat, drink and be merry for tomorrow we die"—the wording that is most familiar today. In modern usage, the ending is often given a jocular twist. As the *New Scientist* put it in an article from 2000, "Eat, drink and be merry, for tomorrow we diet."

The Ends of the Earth

[Deuteronomy 33:17; Job 28:24; Zechariah 9:10]

A very long way away; the back of beyond

Like most other ancient cultures, the ancient Israelites thought it obvious that since the earth was flat it must have limits. "The ends of the earth" therefore appears repeatedly in the Old Testament as a way to describe the furthest reaches of the then-known world. When, in the Book of Job, God is said to "direct his lightning to the ends of the earth," it's just a poetic way of saying that God is in charge everywhere.

Of course, it wasn't long before the ancient Greeks discovered that the earth is in fact not flat but spherical. Not everyone, however, is convinced of the earth's inconvenient roundness. Daniel Shenton, head of the modern Flat Earth Society, gives the Scottish verdict: "Not proven." According to him and his fellow "flat-earthers," the world is a flat disc, centered on the North Pole, surrounded at its Antarctic rim by a wall of ice. The moon landings, he says, and photos showing the round earth hanging in space, were faked. If any ship or aircraft really did fly past the ends of the earth, he says, it would simply fall off the edge and into the infinite abyss below.

An Epiphany

[Matthew 2:1–12]

**A moment of clarity; a sudden understanding
of the truth or meaning of something**

The feast of the Epiphany (from the Greek *epiphainō*, meaning "to appear" or "come to light"), is celebrated on January 6 each year. It marks the moment when the wise men, or "Magi," arrived to worship the baby Jesus in his manger at Bethlehem.

The festival has special significance for Christians because the Magi are non-Jews—this is the moment in the Bible when God reaches out beyond his "chosen people" for the first time.

The modern secular sense of the word has existed since the nineteenth century, although the religious festival has been swallowed up in the UK and the US by the commercial behemoth of Christmas.

Escape by the Skin of One's Teeth

[Job 19:20]

To have a narrow escape

This is one of the many proverbs that owe their origin to the colorful language of the Book of Job. The tormented hero Job is complaining about his woes. He has become, he says, so emaciated that "my bone cleaveth to my skin and to my flesh, and I am escaped with the skin of my teeth."

The proverbial meaning is that he has missed death by a tiny margin—as narrow as the (non-existent) skin on a person's teeth. But biblical scholars have argued endlessly about what the phrase originally signified. Some argue for a more literal interpretation: that Satan kept Job's mouth—the skin of his gums, jaws and lips—healthy in order to encourage him to blaspheme against God.

More recently, the heavy metal band Megadeath put an interesting slant on the saying when they used it as the title for a track on their third album in 1992. Frontman Dave Mustaine explained to a live audience: "This is a song about how many times I tried to kill myself and just couldn't get the job done."

To Every Thing
There Is a Season

[Ecclesiastes 3:1]

**There's a right time and a wrong time
for everything—it's important
to know which is which!**

This handy aphorism is another piece of wisdom from the Book of Ecclesiastes, in which the author offers his thoughts on life, death and what it all means. "To every thing there is a season, and a time to every purpose under the heaven," he writes. Warming to his theme, he continues, there is "a time to kill and a time to heal"; "a time to weep and a time to laugh"; there's even "a time to cast away stones." The full list has twenty-eight different times, and covers eight biblical verses.

With its philosophical and reflective tone, it has become one of the most quoted and most popular passages in the Old Testament, a firm favorite for readings at funerals and other sad occasions. In 1959 the famous words even became a surprise hit when they were set to music by the folk musician Pete Seeger in a song called "Turn! Turn! Turn!" Covered by The Byrds in 1965, the track rocketed to number one on the US singles chart—the iron-age lyrics are by far the oldest words ever to have become a chart-topping hit.

An Eye for an Eye

Punishment fitting the crime; retribution equal to the damage caused

The principle of equal retribution is one of the oldest legal ideas in history, found both in the ancient Babylonian laws of Hammurabi and in the Old Testament. In the Book of Exodus, God tells Moses: "Thou shalt give life for life, eye for eye, tooth for tooth, hand for hand, foot for foot, burning for burning," and "wound for wound."

This so-called *lex talionis* ("law of retribution") does have the virtue of simplicity but it hardly fits with modern ideas about prisoner rehabilitation and human rights. What's more, Jesus famously rejected "an eye for an eye" in his Sermon on the Mount, preferring to turn the other cheek.

However, the ancient code hasn't died out entirely. In 2008, an Iranian man who blinded and disfigured a woman in an acid attack was condemned in a criminal court in Tehran to be blinded himself—giving literal meaning to "eye for an eye" justice.

Eyeless in Gaza

[Judges 16:21]

Blind; helpless; stripped of power

This unusual phrase was made famous by Aldous Huxley, who used it as the title of his best-selling 1936 novel on pacifism. It's an allusion to the story of Samson, an Israelite hero who was granted superhuman strength by God and is famous for, among other things, single-handedly killing a thousand Philistines with nothing but a donkey's jawbone.

The actual wording of the modern phrase comes from Milton, who, in his 1671 poem *Samson Agonistes*, describes the hero after he has finally been captured and blinded by the Philistines. Samson laments bitterly:

> Ask for this great deliverer now and find him
> Eyeless in Gaza at the mill with slaves,
> Himself in bonds under Philistian yoke.

In modern times, the phrase is almost exclusively used by grateful headline writers tackling the thorny issue of the Gaza Strip. Since the news from that part of the world tends reliably towards the somber, "Eyeless in Gaza" is rarely far off the mark.

Samson and Delilah

Samson, whose story is told in the Book of Judges, was the ultimate biblical macho-man—lion-killer, slayer of Philistines, and rampant womanizer. That, however, would prove his undoing. His last conquest was a woman called Delilah, from the valley of Sorek. The Philistines, long since having despaired of killing Samson by conventional means, decided a subtler approach was in order, and bribed Delilah to find out and betray the source of Samson's superhuman strength.

The first few times Delilah asked, Samson fobbed her off with fake answers. She would try whatever magic he suggested (binding him in new rope, winding twigs around his limbs) but each time she alarmed him, announcing that the Philistines had arrived, he would shake off his shackles and be as potent as ever.

You'd think, after the third time this happened, Samson might have smelled a rat. It's a testament to Delilah's powers as a seductress that instead he finally revealed to her his real secret: no razor had ever touched his hair, which was consecrated to the Lord. That night, Samson woke up bald, bound and surrounded. His heroic career was over.

(He did have one final flourish though. One evening, his Philistine captors brought him to a feast to mock him. In a last burst of strength, Samson ripped the two central pillars out of the palace, collapsing the walls and killing himself along with three thousand Philistine men, women and children, which the Bible regards as a very creditable score.)

Fall from Grace

[Galatians 5:4; see also Genesis 3]

To fall out of favor or lose one's status

This phrase first occurs in the Bible in St. Paul's Letter to the Galatians, who have begun to stray from the true path of Christianity. The sharp-tongued apostle quickly fires off a stinging rebuke: "Christ is become of no effect unto you . . ." he writes furiously. "Ye are fallen from grace."

There could be no greater statement of displeasure. "Grace," in this context, meant all hope of divine love and forgiveness. And the Greek word translated as "fall" can also mean to be "thrown overboard," "exiled" or "booed off stage."

But the idea of "the fall" in Christian thought goes back much further than a bunch of misbehaving Galatians. In fact, the most famous "fall from grace" (although it isn't called by that name in the Bible) was the expulsion of Adam and Eve from the Garden of Eden. Even today, a condition of unusual innocence or purity can be described as "prelapsarian"—"from before the fall."

As a phrase, "fall from grace" is commonly used today in contexts ranging from the spiritual (it was used as a title for a 2007 film about a renegade Baptist preacher) to the profane (a 1988 album by the Pogues, led by their chronically intoxicated front man Shane MacGowan). It even, bizarrely, is the name of a quest in the popular online game *World of Warcraft*.

Fall on Stony Ground

[Matthew 13:3–8; Mark 4:3–8]

**To meet with an unresponsive audience;
fall on deaf ears**

In the Gospels, Jesus tells the story of a man who went to sow some seed: "As he sowed, some fell by the wayside, and the fowls of the air came and devoured it up. And some fell on stony ground, where it had not much earth . . . when the sun was up, it was scorched; and because it had no root, it withered away." Only a few seeds fall on fertile soil and flourish.

Of course, the man in the parable represents Jesus himself, the seed is his preaching, and various patches of ground—whether fertile or stony—are the hearts of men.

Although it's not the most colorful of Jesus' stories, this parable has given us as many as three separate expressions that are still in use. Anything that gets discarded can be said to have "fallen by the wayside"; an appeal that is ignored has "fallen on stony ground"; and some ideas find "fertile ground" and really take off. This last, sadly, is most often heard today when places are described as "fertile ground for extremism."

The Fat of the Land

....

[Genesis 45:18]

The best agricultural produce

The Book of Genesis tells the story of Joseph, who was sold into slavery by his brothers but ends up as the highest official in the court of the Egyptian pharaoh. Years later,

---

Joseph

Even before it was an Andrew Lloyd Webber musical, the story of Joseph was always a biblical favorite. It starts in a sleepy village in Canaan, where the aging patriarch Jacob dotes on his young son Joseph and gives him a special colorful coat to wear. Not surprisingly, this favoritism goes down pretty badly with Joseph's eleven dowdier brothers, although their response is a little extreme. After attacking him and keeping him in a hole in the ground for a while, they sell young Joseph into slavery, bringing his torn and bloodied coat back to Jacob to convince him his son is dead.

It need hardly be said, however, that God has a plan all along. Joseph winds up in Egypt, where he successfully predicts a famine by interpreting one of the pharaoh's dreams. This foresight saves Egypt, and the pharaoh rewards Joseph with wealth and power beyond his wildest imagination.

---

his brothers come to Egypt themselves to buy corn from Joseph, whom they do not recognize. After much going back and forth, Joseph's secret identity is revealed and his brothers and father are invited to stay in Egypt as honored guests of the pharaoh himself. "Lade your beasts," says the mighty monarch, "and take your father and your households, and come unto me . . . and ye shall eat the fat of the land."

It's an odd phrase to modern ears, but at the time of the King James translation in the early seventeenth century, the fat was considered the most desirable part of any meat. Indeed, even the Victorians still bred cattle to produce as much fat as possible, rather than, as we do today, insisting on eating nothing but lean muscle.

So when the translators wrote "the fat of the land," the idea was not that the land would be literally oozing lipids. Instead, "fat" was used metaphorically, to signify "the best bit" or "the choice produce."

Feet of Clay

[Daniel 2:32-45]

A serious defect discovered in someone of high reputation or standing

This unusual-sounding phrase comes from a dream of the Babylonian King Nebuchadnezzar, who sees the image of a huge figure in his sleep. "The image's head was of fine gold, his breast and his arms of silver, his belly and his thighs of brass, his legs of iron, his feet part of iron and part of clay."

All of a sudden, a giant stone appears out of nowhere, smashes the fragile feet and brings the whole statue tumbling down.

The prophet Daniel, who is brought in to interpret this extraordinary vision, explains that the giant figure represents the kingdoms of men, declining in quality until they are finally smashed to pieces by God—the mysterious rock.

In 1814, Byron stole the biblical story in his *Ode to Napoleon*, which gives rise to the modern meaning of the phrase. Napoleon had just been defeated by the British and their allies, and had been sent into exile on Elba. Such leaders, writes Byron, are idols, with "fronts of brass and feet of clay."

Of course, Byron was too quick to gloat over Napoleon's fall. In 1815, the Emperor was back in Europe, and came close to defeating a combined Prussian-British army at the battle of Waterloo. Nevertheless, searching for the "feet of clay" hidden by the golden reputations of great men and women remains a favorite human pastime, particularly beloved by tabloid journalists.

Fight the Good Fight

[1 Timothy 6:12]

Keep on working in a good cause

In a world full of hostile pagans and murderous Roman emperors, the early Christians soon found that keeping the faith could easily involve dying. And it wasn't long before Christians got pretty good at killing, too. It should be no surprise then that the first Christian writings, as found in the New Testament, have more than their share of martial and soldierly metaphors.

This one comes from another of St. Paul's letters, advising his follower Timothy on the best way to advance the Christian cause. Above all, says Paul, "fight the good fight of faith."

Over the following centuries, everyone from the Crusaders to the Salvation Army followed in Timothy's footsteps, fighting the "good fight" in ways that varied from the spiritual to the painfully literal. "Fight the good fight" was also the title of a favorite hymn written by the Irish clergyman John Monsell in 1863, which further popularized the phrase, especially when it was used in the soundtrack for the Oscar-winning 1981 drama *Chariots of Fire*.

A Fig Leaf

[Genesis 3:7]

**A flimsy pretext or covering for some
shameful act**

The crime of Adam and Eve, says the Book of Genesis,
was to eat the forbidden fruit from the grandly named
"tree of the knowledge of good and evil." The Bible records that as soon as the two miscreant mortals tasted its
fruit, "their eyes were opened."

This sudden awakening brought an uncomfortable re-
alization. Like a pair of energetic sleepwalkers, mankind's
first ancestors had been wandering around all this time
entirely in the nude. Given the circumstances—for example the imminent arrival of a very angry deity—one
might think that Eve and Adam would have had more
pressing concerns than mere modesty, but Genesis is very
clear in its account. The first thing they did after eating
the fruit was to sit down and construct themselves some
makeshift underwear out of fig leaves.

Thousands of years later, clergymen who were con-
cerned about excessive nudity in classical and Renaissance art were inspired by Adam and Eve's example.
Without access to censors' blackout bars, or pixelation,
they adopted the tasteful strategy of painting over the in-
decent parts of painted nudes with conveniently placed
fig leaves. This sense of thinly covering up some shameful
secret is still preserved today.

Fire and Brimstone

[Genesis 19:24; Psalm 11:6; Isaiah 34:9;
Ezekiel 38:22; Revelation 21:8]

Angry or terrifying words, especially as
part of a sermon

There's a school of thought, championed by Sigmund Freud in his 1939 book *Moses and Monotheism*, that says that the Hebrew Yahweh originally started life as a volcano god. You can see where the great psychiatrist might have got that impression. The Almighty is undeniably fond of appearing in pillars of smoke, or on fiery mountaintops. He spoke to Moses from a burning bush.

Most of all, when he gets angry, his preferred strategy is to shake the Earth and start hurling fire and brimstone. Brimstone, of course, better known as sulfur, is a common by-product of volcanic eruptions.

After making their biblical debut at the destruction of Sodom and Gomorrah, fire and brimstone quickly became a favorite metaphor among English writers for the overwhelming power of divine wrath. The Puritan Thomas Vincent wrote a book called *Fire and Brimstone in Hell* after witnessing the Great Fire of London in 1666. The Protestant pastors of the eighteenth-century Great Awakening were so fond of threatening their congregations with eternal damnation that they became known as the "fire and brimstone preachers"—giving rise to the modern usage of the phrase.

A Fleshpot

[Exodus 16:3]

**A place of vice and luxury; something with
sensual allure**

In the Book of Exodus, Moses leads the Hebrews out of
Egypt to escape from the tyrannical pharaoh and find
the Promised Land. They follow him eagerly enough at
first, but it soon becomes clear that the journey will be far
from straightforward. As geography students will remember, between Egypt and Israel lies the barren wasteland of
the Sinai Desert.

It isn't long before Moses' flock start complaining:
"Would to God we had died by the hand of the Lord in
the land of Egypt," they moan, "when we sat by the flesh
pots, and when we did eat bread to the full."

"Flesh pots," in this passage, means exactly what it
sounds like: pots in which you cook flesh. But the fleshpots of Egypt became a popular metaphor for any luxuri-
ous scene imagined with regret or disapproval. Gradually,
the Egyptian reference dropped away—in 1710, Jonathan Swift writes of the "fleshpots of Cavan Street"—
until fleshpot became an all-purpose word for anywhere
that was particularly alluring. These days a "fleshpot"
can be anything from a casino in Las Vegas to a London
nightclub.

Forbidden Fruit

[Genesis 2:16–17]

Something that's tempting but not allowed

When God creates Adam, in the Book of Genesis, he puts him in the Garden of Eden as master of all he surveys. There's only one rule: "But of the tree of the knowledge of good and evil," which stands in the middle of the Garden, "thou shalt not eat of it: for in the day that thou eatest thereof thou shalt surely die."

With that setup, the ending is inevitable. Adam and Eve eat the fruit (an apple in Christian tradition, although in Islam it's thought to have been a banyan, and some scholars now suggest the pomegranate). God—being omniscient—catches them at it, and expels them from the Garden.

His parting words are an extraordinary poetic summing-up of the human condition, and worth quoting in full: "Cursed is the ground for thy sake; in sorrow shalt thou eat of it all the days of thy life . . . In the sweat of thy face shalt thou eat bread, till thou return unto the ground; for out of it wast thou taken: for dust thou art, and unto dust shalt thou return."

In theology, Adam and Eve's disobedience is known as the "original sin," and dooms mankind to a mortal and imperfect existence, redeemed only by the sacrifice of Jesus, thousands of years later.

The Fruit of One's Loins

[Genesis 30:2; Luke 1:42; Acts 2:30]

One's children

The word "fruit" appears frequently in the Bible in the sense of "children." "Fruit" could originally mean any kind of produce—the fruit of a tree might be apples and pears. Fruits of the earth are vegetables. Children, therefore, are the "fruit of the body" or, as the Book of Acts has it, "the fruit of your loins."

This use of fruit was common in English until at least the mid-nineteenth century. Anyone in the habit of saying Hail Marys would have been used to quoting Luke's Gospel: "Blessed art thou among women and blessed is the fruit of thy womb." An 1834 medical textbook could talk straight-facedly about the dangers of losing the "uterine fruit" during the "period of parturition" (losing one's baby while giving birth).

In today's less religious atmosphere, however, the phrase is almost never used without a gentle dose of irony; "Gwyneth Paltrow and Chris Martin are expecting a second fruit of their loins," reported one 2007 gossip writer. Their first child's name, of course, was Apple.

One little-used modern descendant of the biblical phrase has lost its high-sounding connotations. A child whose parents love to show it off, says the online Urban Dictionary, is sarcastically known as a "loin trophy."

Gall and Wormwood

[Deuteronomy 29:18]

**Something bitter; an unpleasant feeling
or experience**

Deuteronomy describes Israelites who worship false gods as "a root that beareth gall and wormwood," and wormwood has been proverbially associated with bitterness and unpleasantness ever since. Roald Dahl called a mean-spirited teacher Mr. Wormwood in his 1988 novel *Matilda*. C. S. Lewis gave the same name to a junior devil in the *Screwtape Letters* (1942). And in J. K. Rowling's Harry Potter novels, the plant is a crucial ingredient in a potion called "The Draught of Living Death."

The pithiest expression, however, is from *The Cruise of the Cachalot*, an 1898 novel by Frank T. Bullen: "The sight of other people's good fortune is gall and wormwood."

So what is this "wormwood" that gets such a bad name? Scientists call it *Artemisia absinthium*, a bitter herb native to Europe and the Mediterranean—*absinthium*, in Greek, literally means "undrinkable."

Of course, *absinthium* is also the key ingredient in absinthe, the "Green Fairy," one of the world's most notorious alcoholic drinks.

Get Thee Behind Me, Satan

[Luke 4:8; Matthew 16:3; Mark 8:33]

"Don't tempt me!"

This phrase is a reference to the Temptation of Christ, a period of forty days and forty nights in which Jesus wandered alone in the wilderness, and the Devil tempts him to break his faith with God. Jesus replies: "Get thee behind me, Satan. For it is written: Thou shalt worship the Lord thy God, and him only shalt thou serve."

Jesus' famous reply is still used as a jocular response to any offer that is tempting but sinful. But although the phrase is well-established in modern English, its biblical roots are less sturdy and straightforward than they might appear.

For one thing, several ancient texts of Luke's Gospel leave out the words entirely—suggesting they may have been a later addition. In fact, the one place where the words can reliably be found is much later in Jesus' story, when he says "Get thee behind me, Satan" to his disciple St. Peter.

But he's not calling Peter the devil. The Hebrew word *sātān* originally meant "an adversary" or "one who opposes," and Peter has just been opposing—understandably enough—Jesus' intention to go to Jerusalem and endure crucifixion and death. When Jesus calls Peter "Satan," he's telling him off for arguing, not comparing him to the Prince of Darkness.

To Gird One's Loins

....

[2 Kings 4:29; 1 Peter 1:13]

To prepare, especially for something strenuous

Two archaic words come together in this phrase. "Gird," from the Old English *gyrdan,* means to put a belt (or girdle) around something. Loins, from the Latin *lumbus,* originally described the flanks of an animal and, from the fourteenth century, those parts of the human body which, as medieval writers primly put it, "should be covered."

In biblical times, when long robes were still in fashion, anyone embarking on strenuous physical activity or going into battle ran a serious risk of tripping on a trailing hem and falling flat on their face. The solution? To tuck one's robe into one's belt, i.e. to gird one's loins. The phrase, in this literal sense, occurs frequently in the Bible, starting from the Second Book of Kings.

The phrase can also be found in the Bible as a metaphor, in the First Epistle of Peter. "Gird up the loins of your mind," writes the apostle to his followers—an awkward image, but he got his point across.

Give Someone the Evil Eye

[Mark 7:22; Matthew 5:29]

**Curse someone, or stare at someone
with hatred**

In Mark's Gospel, Jesus lists the vices of mankind. Most are predictable enough: "thefts, covetousness, wickedness, deceit, lasciviousness, blasphemy, pride, foolishness." But one item on the list stands out: "an evil eye."

Theologians have interpreted this "evil eye" to mean something like "malice" or "envy," but it's possible to take the idea more literally. In fact, in Matthew's Gospel Jesus tells his followers: "If thy right eye offend thee, pluck it out." You'd certainly want to be sure it was your eye, rather than your mind, that was the problem.

At any rate, the idea of a literal evil eye has been widespread in cultures across the world, from the earliest civilizations. At the height of the witch-hunting panic in early modern Europe, thousands of unfortunate old ladies were burned or drowned for "cursing" their neighbors with a malicious look.

In modern speech, the evil eye is a less common phrase than it used to be, but the idea lives on in a teenage catchphrase recently made famous by Vicky Pollard, from the BBC Television comedy *Little Britain*: "Stop giving me evils!"

Give Up the Ghost

[Job 14:10; Mark 15:37; Acts 12:23]

To die

The Acts of the Apostles has a grisly account of the death of the notorious King Herod Agrippa, who had been persecuting the disciples after Jesus' death. "The angel of the Lord smote him," says the Bible (with a hint of satisfaction). "He was eaten of worms, and gave up the ghost."

Later writers identified the disease as a much-feared condition called *Morbus pedicularis*. Sufferers were eaten alive by lice growing in ulcers beneath the skin and died in excruciating agony.

The most famous biblical use of the phrase, however, is in the dramatic description of the last moments of Jesus on the cross. Mark's Gospel says that, after hours of suffering, he "cried with a loud voice, and gave up the ghost and the veil of the temple was rent in twain from the top to the bottom."

The "ghost"—a translation of the Greek word *psychë*—is simply the soul or spirit (not, as in modern English, something spooky), and "give up the ghost" is often used today as a poetic way of saying that someone died. It is commonly used in a jocular fashion to describe the "deaths" of machines or appliances.

Go from Strength to Strength

[Psalm 84:7]

**To progress from one success to another;
to be on a roll**

The Book of Psalms describes pilgrims arriving in Jerusalem: "They go from strength to strength. Every one of them in Zion appeareth before God."

The unspoken contrast is with the exiled Jews, forcibly deported to Babylon by the Babylonian King Nebuchadnezzar in the sixth century BC. This was actually a fairly common way of pacifying rebels in the ancient Middle East. The Assyrians (who started the trend) had been shuffling populations around their vast empire since the thirteenth century BC.

Like the ancient Israelites, this fragment of their song has also moved a long way from its roots. In the modern world, "from strength to strength" has become an indispensable cliché of "journalese," applied to everything from the world economy to local five-a-side soccer teams. In the 1980s the phrase even enjoyed a brief period of fame as a slogan for Peugeot cars, which, referring to their famous lion logo, grandly proclaimed: "The lion leaps from strength to strength."

Go the Way of All Flesh

[Joshua 23:14; 1 Kings 2:2]

To die

The Book of Joshua records how the prophet, growing old, gathered his people together for one last farewell speech. "Behold!" he tells them. "This day I am going the way of all the earth." King David uses the same poetic phrase when saying goodbye to his son, Solomon, and the idea is plain—death is common to all "earthly" (as opposed to "heavenly") creatures, so there's no point making a fuss over it.

In modern usage, "earth" is almost always replaced with "flesh." Both are standard biblical images for what is mortal rather than spiritual, and "the way of all flesh" was made famous by the writer Samuel Butler, who used it as the title for his famous autobiographical novel of 1903.

But "flesh" adds an extra sense of sinfulness and carnal desire as well as mortality. The first occurrence of the modern form of the phrase dates from *Westward Ho!,* a Jacobean satire by John Webster and Thomas Dekker, published in 1607. The authors' line plays on the double meaning: " 'Saw you my uncle?' 'I saw him even now going the way of all flesh, that's to say, towards the kitchen.' "

Go to Jericho

[2 Samuel 10:5]

**An impolite command to leave;
like "Go to Hell!"**

This old-fashioned phrase comes from an odd incident in the Second Book of Samuel. King David sends ambassadors to the heathen King Hanun, but as soon as they arrive they are accused of spying and sent home again. As a parting insult, Hanun shaves off half of each one's beard and cuts their robes off at the waist, leaving their most delicate parts exposed to public ridicule.

"The men," records Samuel, "were greatly ashamed," so David allowed them to "tarry in Jericho" (just north of the Dead Sea) until they could be rid of their enforced facial topiary. Ever since, Jericho has been used proverbially to mean anywhere out of the way or secluded.

The expression was common in the nineteenth century (used, for example, in Thackeray's 1858 novel *The Virginians*). In the diary of the eighteenth-century clergyman James Woodforde, Jericho even appears as a euphemism for an outhouse toilet—a terrible fate for a city that is thought to be the oldest human settlement on earth, inhabited for as long as twelve thousand years.

The Walls of Jericho

As well as being earth's oldest continuously inhabited city, Jericho was also—the Bible says—the site of one of the strangest sieges in the history of war. The story goes that Joshua, leading the Israelites into the Promised Land after the Exodus, found his way blocked by the great walls of Jericho. Luckily, God was on hand with a plan.

Following instructions, Joshua surrounded the city and for six days held a procession round the walls, with a troop of trumpet-playing priests leading the way and the Ark of the Covenant following behind. On the seventh day, after this prolonged aural assault, the Israelite army followed their regular fanfare with a great shout, the noise from which brought the mighty defenses crumbling down.

A Good Samaritan

[Luke 10:25–37]

Someone who helps in time of need

The parable of the Good Samaritan, in Luke's Gospel, tells of a traveler who is attacked by thieves on the notoriously bandit-ridden road from Jerusalem to Jericho. Bleeding by the roadside, he is ignored first by a priest and then by a Levite (a member of the tribe of Levi, who traditionally had a special religious role among the Israelites). Finally, a member of the hated sect of Samaritans stops, tends the traveler's wounds, and escorts him to a nearby inn to recover from his ordeal.

The metaphorical use of "Samaritan" to mean a charitable person who helps those in need has existed in English since the seventeenth century and has been common since then. In 1953 a London vicar took the story as his inspiration in setting up a charity called The Samaritans, which provides a helpline for people contemplating suicide.

Meanwhile, in the Middle East, around seven hundred descendants of the biblical Samaritans are still clinging on. Claiming to be the only true adherents of Judaism (mainstream Judaism, they claim, was corrupted during the Babylonian exile), they live in tight-knit communities in Israel and the West Bank and still observe the ancient religion of their forefathers.

A Hail Mary Pass

[Luke 1:28]

In American football, a long forward pass with little hope of success; generally, a long-shot

The Hail Mary, or *Ave Maria*, is one of the most famous prayers in Christian history. It has its roots in the Gospel of Luke, when the angel Gabriel announces to the Virgin

Mary that she is going to give birth to the son of God.

"Hail, thou that art highly favored," says the archangel. "The Lord is with thee. Blessed art thou among women." In the Middle Ages, these words evolved into the familiar prayer of today, which is said ten times as part of the Catholic rosary:

> Hail Mary, full of grace, the Lord is with thee;
> Blessed art thou amongst women,
> And blessed is the fruit of thy womb, Jesus.
> Holy Mary, Mother of God, Pray for us sinners, now
> And at the hour of our death.
> Amen.

The modern phrase, however, has a much shorter history. In 1975, Dallas Cowboys quarterback Roger Staubach made headlines by throwing an extraordinarily long game-winning pass in the final seconds of a crucial play-off against the Minnesota Vikings. When asked how he did it he told reporters: "I closed my eyes and said a Hail Mary."

Hallelujah

[Psalms, e.g. 106:48, 111; Revelation 19:1]

An expression of joy, sometimes sarcastic

"Hallelujah" is a simple transliteration of the Hebrew *halle˘lu˘ yāh,* where *yāh* is the name of God and *halle˘lu˘* an imperative form of the verb "to praise." Like "Hosanna" (meaning "help us we pray"), it is a single word that sums up the whole Christian celebration of God.

John Milton imagines it as the song of the heavenly choirs in *Paradise Lost* (1667): "the Empyrean rung with Hallelujahs." Walter Scott had "eternal hallelujahs" as the opposite of "eternal lamentations" in *Tales of My Landlord* (1818).

The word is most familiar today for its impact on later Protestant churches, especially in America, where repeated exclamations of "Hallelujah!" are delivered with particular dramatic gusto. The Canadian singer Leonard Cohen gave his own take on the word with his much-covered 1984 track of the same name.

These days, "Hallelujah" is a bit strong for everyday speech. When people say it now, they're unlikely to be totally straight-faced.

To Harden One's Heart

[Exodus 7–11]

**To become less compassionate, often
preparing to resist some request**

The Book of Exodus finds the Israelites trapped in Egypt, captives of the pharaoh. One day Moses and Aaron, the Hebrew leaders, go to Pharaoh and ask him—in the

Ten Plagues of Egypt

When Pharaoh refuses to let Moses and Aaron leave Egypt, God sends ten plagues against the Egyptians to help change the monarch's mind and to demonstrate his power:

1. The rivers of Egypt are turned to blood.
2. Egypt suffers an invasion of frogs, which crawl all over the Egyptians' beds and eyes and "kneadingtroughs."
3. All the dust of Egypt becomes a swarm of lice.
4. Clouds of flies corrupt all the land.
5. All the cattle in Egypt die of disease.
6. An outbreak of crippling boils.
7. Egypt is stricken with deadly downpours of hail mixed with fire.
8. Hordes of locusts descend on the land and eat all the crops.
9. Things start getting even more sinister as an inky blackness engulfs the country for three days.
10. By this point, God is getting seriously wrathful. Time for the big guns. One night, he reaches out and personally smites every single firstborn child in Egypt, killing them all.

Finally, Pharaoh gets the message. Moses and the Israelites are allowed to depart, leaving Egypt ruined behind them.

words later made famous as a Negro spiritual—to "let my people go."

Despite their pleas, Pharaoh refuses. Bad choice. The consequences of his stubbornness were the plagues of Egypt, which included the slaughter of every Egyptian firstborn child, and the destruction of the entire Egyptian army.

But Pharaoh, as the last of these calamities engulfed him, would have been entitled to think he'd had a raw deal. God, after all, in an act of cruel sabotage, had "hardened Pharaoh's heart, that he hearkened not unto them." He made Pharaoh choose wrong, and then punished him for it.

In modern usage, hardening one's heart usually involves an element of self-fortification, in anticipation of a trial. A song called "Harden My Heart" by Quarterflash hit the *Billboard* charts in 1982.

To Have the Patience of Job

[Job 1–3; James 5:11]

To be long-suffering; to endure hardship bravely

This phrase, a quotation from the Epistle of St. James, refers to the story of Job, whose faith was famously tested by God in the Old Testament. Job endured disease, the loss of his crops and his herds, and even the deaths of his sons and daughters, without ever cursing his creator. "The Lord gave, and the Lord hath taken away," he says philosophically. "Blessed be the name of the Lord."

His story is one of the first biblical passages to touch on the famous "problem of evil" that has troubled theologians since the first days of Christianity. The question is—if the world is created by an omnipotent and benevolent deity, why is it so full of pain and suffering? Christians have found many ways to answer the question over the years, often attributing evil to the abuse of human free will or to the corrupting influence of Adam and Eve's "original sin" (eating the Forbidden Fruit in the Garden of Eden). In the end, however, the best answer may be the simplest: "God moves in mysterious ways."

He Who Increases Knowledge Increases Sorrow

[Ecclesiastes 1:18]

The more you know the unhappier you'll be

This proverb is one of many nuggets of wisdom from the Book of Ecclesiastes. "In much wisdom is much grief," writes the author, "and he that increaseth knowledge increaseth sorrow." If, as tradition records, the author of Ecclesiastes is the famously intelligent King Solomon, he'd have every reason to know what he was talking about.

It's a pessimistic view, and not one that everyone would agree with. Interestingly though, a 2011 scientific study by Von Helversen et al. in the *Journal of Abnormal Psychiatry* did show a link between knowledge and sorrow—but the chain of cause and effect seemed to be the wrong way round, with unhappiness increasing knowledge. Test subjects in a depressed state of mind actually performed better in analytical tasks than their cheerier friends.

Either way, the expression these days is rarely heard. Much more common is its pithier counterpart, invented by the poet Thomas Gray in 1742 in his "Ode on a Distant Prospect of Eton College": "Ignorance is bliss."

The Heart's Desire

[Romans 10:1]

A person's greatest wish; something longed for

In the Bible, the heart is the seat of the emotions and of the spirit. The word is sometimes even used to mean "soul." The "heart's desire," as found in St. Paul's Epistle to the Romans, is something that is longed for with the very core of a person's being.

The heart hasn't always been thought of as the center

of our emotions, however. The stomach, for example, was once thought to be the source of courage. The kidneys were thought to produce affectionate feelings. The ancient Greeks, meanwhile, thought all our passions came from the liver.

Of course, scientifically speaking, the heart is just a very fancy blood pump, and has nothing to do with feelings at all. The idea probably derives from the fact that strong emotions can cause the release of the hormone adrenalin, which makes the heart beat faster, leading to the illusion that it's the heart itself that is doing the feeling.

To Hide One's Talent Under a Bushel

[Matthew 5:15; Matthew 25:14–30]

To waste or conceal one's natural gifts

This odd phrase derives from the names of two old-fashioned units of measurement: A bushel was a measure of volume, equal to four "pecks." The word could also mean a basket that contained precisely a bushel's worth. A talent, meanwhile, was an ancient unit of weight, and therefore came to describe a valuable coin, worth one talent of gold or silver. Although the value varied over the centuries, a talent was always a significant sum of money.

So how did these two combine in modern language? The phrase actually results from a confusion between two biblical allegories. In the first, Jesus tells his followers to let their light "shine before men," for "neither do men light a candle, and put it under a bushel but on a candlestick; and it giveth light unto all that are in the house."

The second is more complicated: a man goes travelling, leaving his fortune of several talents divided among his servants. Two of the servants invest their portion and are able to show a healthy profit when their master returns. The third, trying to play it safe, buries his talent underground.

If he thinks this caution will earn him praise, he is sadly mistaken. In an unforgettable (and much quoted) line, the master orders: "Cast ye the unprofitable servant into outer darkness: there shall be weeping and gnashing of teeth." One dreads to think what would have happened to the servant if he had invested his talent in sub-prime mortgages.

Holier Than Thou

[Isaiah 65:5]

**Ostentatiously pious or virtuous;
snobbish and hypocritical**

In the Book of Isaiah, the prophet speaks of a "rebellious people" who say: "Stand by thyself; come not near to me, for I am holier than thou." These, he says rather oddly, are "a smoke in God's nose."

Later Christians sometimes regard this passage as a prophetic description of the Pharisees, who used, apparently, to be so squeamish about mingling with lesser folk that if they even brushed against a commoner's clothes they'd be forced to "dip themselves all over."

The phrase became popular in English in the twentieth century, as people rebelled against the moralizing of their Victorian ancestors. Taking that spirit of rebellion to an extreme, the heavy-metal band Metallica used the quote as a title for a track on their 1991 *Black Album*, attacking social hypocrisy through the ever-popular medium of shouty vocals and a distorted electric guitar.

A House Divided Against Itself Cannot Stand

[Matthew 12:25]

Without unity there can be no strength

In Matthew's Gospel, Jesus tells a crowd of impudent Pharisees, "Every kingdom divided against itself is brought to desolation; and every city or house divided against itself shall not stand."

However, the phrase didn't enter the modern lexicon

until it was memorably quoted by Abraham Lincoln in his famous nomination acceptance speech of 1858. Addressing the contentious issue of slavery in the United States, he told an audience of Republican politicians that "a house divided against itself cannot stand. I believe this government cannot endure, permanently half slave and half free."

His words were prophetic. Three years later, the US government did indeed split, and the resulting civil war between slave and free states cost more than six hundred thousand lives. The phrase meanwhile, became famous, immortalized as the title of a 1913 movie, a 1935 novel, and, rather grandiosely, an episode of the hit TV series *Dallas*. Not exactly what Jesus had in mind.

How Are the Mighty Fallen

....

[Samuel 1:19–27]

**Those who were once powerful are
now humbled**

These days, people tend to say "how are the mighty fallen" out of smugness rather than sympathy. Confronted by the sight of the "mighty" laid low, only the saintliest souls can resist a shameful flicker of pleasure—that strange emotion so perfectly captured by the German word *schadenfreude.*

In the Bible, though, the phrase has no such unworthy undertones. Instead, it appears as a repeated refrain in the poetic lament of David for his fallen companion Jonathan, the son of Saul.

"The beauty of Israel is slain upon thy high places," complains the stricken prince. "How are the mighty fallen! . . . Ye mountains of Gilboa, let there be no dew, neither let there be rain, upon you . . . How are the mighty fallen, and the weapons of war perished!"

The Victorian novelist Thomas Hardy put this beautiful and tragic Bible passage to good use in his 1891 masterpiece *Tess of the D'Urbervilles.* John Durbeyfield, the impoverished ne'er-do-well who is Tess's father, has a chance encounter with a wandering genealogist and learns that his distant forebears were the aristocratic D'Urbervilles, since fallen on hard times. This sudden discovery of hereditary grandeur sets John and his family on the road to catastrophe. Much later in the book, after John's death, his tombstone is engraved with a bitterly ironic epitaph: "How are the Mighty Fallen."

I Am What I Am

[Exodus 3:14]

**I accept my identity and am not
going to change**

In modern thought, the path to happiness lies in self-acceptance. Thousands of self-help books tell us to love ourselves for who we really are. The mantra? "I am what I am." Pop songs reinforce the message. "I am what I am. I do what I want," sang Dido in her 1999 hit "Here With Me." Shirley Bassey and Merle Haggard are among several artists to have released whole albums with "I am what I am" as the title.

In English usage, the phrase goes back through Oscar Wilde ("I am what I am. There is nothing more to be said," *The Picture of Dorian Gray*, 1891) to a Jacobean tragedy called *Cupid's Revenge* that was published in 1615.

Whether they know it or not, Wilde, Dido and company are quoting the Bible. In Exodus, Moses asks God to tell him his name. God replies: "I AM THAT I AM."

Needless to say, this cryptic answer has been occupying theologians and philosophers ever since. Some say it's a promise to stay faithful to the Israelites ("I will be what I have always been"). Others claim that it's a statement about the ineffable nature of divine existence.

A Jeremiad

[Jeremiah 1:10; Lamentations]

A fierce tirade against something; a lamentation

The prophet Jeremiah has a good claim to be seen as the Bible's gloomiest holy figure. From the moment when God first spoke to him as a child, his mission was clear: "I have this day set thee over the nations and over the kingdoms, to root out, and to pull down, and to destroy, and to throw down."

In the Book of Jeremiah, the prophet carries out his instructions with aplomb. His message was a dire warning: The people of Judah had sinned against God and so God was going to destroy them, subjecting them to the oppression of the Babylonians.

At the time, this was not a popular view. At one point, he was thrown into a dungeon by the Judaean king to prevent him from damaging military morale. But of course he turned out to have been right: Jerusalem did fall to Babylon, and the nation of Judah was overthrown. According to tradition, Jeremiah then retired to a cave to write the Book of Lamentations, which is about as cheery as it sounds.

The modern usage of the phrase tends to side with the king over the prophet. To describe someone's work as a "jeremiad" usually implies that it goes too far. The phrase originally applied only to written works, but today it can be used for anything from a full-length book to an angry radio interview.

A Jeroboam

[1 Kings 11:26–40 and 14:16]

A very large bottle of wine, holding 3 liters, or as much as four ordinary bottles

Jeroboam was a king of the ten northern tribes of Israel, which split off from the southern Kingdom of Judah after the reign of King Solomon. He is best remembered for having set up two golden calves for his people to worship, which, as any biblical scholar could have told him, was a very bad idea. Last time the Israelites had tried it, under Moses in the Sinai desert, God was so angry that it took the wholesale slaughter of twenty-three thousand men followed by a devastating plague, just to appease him.

This time, God punished Jeroboam by causing him to suffer a crushing defeat in battle against the Judeans. According to the Bible, half a million of his soldiers died, and Jeroboam's power was shattered.

Despite this mishap, Jeroboam has managed to be remembered in an at least jokingly positive light. When nineteenth-century wags were deciding what to call their latest vast wine bottle, they thought of Jeroboam, a "mighty man of valor . . . who made Israel to sin" (1 Kings 14:16).

A Jezebel

....

[1 Kings 16:31 and 21:25; 2 Kings 9]

A "wicked" woman; a prostitute

The biblical Jezebel was a Phoenician princess who married King Ahab of Israel and quickly became notorious. Gaudy and glamorous, she converted her husband to the pagan worship of Baal, persecuted Jewish prophets, and generally exerted much more political influence than was thought seemly for a mere woman.

Eventually, as recorded in the Second Book of Kings, God arranges a military coup and Jezebel is thrown out of a window by her own eunuchs and her body eaten by dogs. As God had grimly told his prophets: "The carcase of Jezebel shall be as dung upon the face of the field."

In 1558, the clergyman John Knox continued the defilement of Jezebel's memory when he used the dead queen as a symbol of feminine wickedness. His pamphlet was called *The First Blast of the Trumpet Against the Monstrous Regiment of Women* and said that God had "raised up Jezebels" to be "the foremost of his plagues." A 1938 Bette Davis film called *Jezebel* told the story of a woman whose "outrageous" behavior costs her the one she loves. As late as the 1963, an advice columnist in the *Windsor Star* could talk about the urgency of getting girls with "Jezebel syndrome" into the hands of psychiatrists as soon as possible.

It's not all bad for Jezebel though. As the feminist movement grew through the twentieth century, Jezebel was often taken up not as a villain but as a heroine—a biblical pioneer of women's lib.

A Jonathan

[2 Samuel 1:26]

An American

A "Jonathan" is an old-fashioned term for an American, equivalent to "John Bull" for an Englishman. It comes from a story about George Washington, who, when he ran out of ammunition, said "we must consult Brother Jonathan."

"Brother Jonathan" is a quote from David's lament in the Second Book of Samuel, but the Jonathan that Washington meant was Jonathan Trumbull, the Governor of Connecticut.

Trumbull duly supplied the ammunition, and "Brother Jonathan" became a symbolic name for America itself, like the later "Uncle Sam."

The poet James Lowell used the phrase in 1848 to sum up the difference between Englishmen and Americans: "An abstract idea will do for Jonathan," he wrote, but "To move John [Bull], you must make your fulcrum of solid beef and pudding."

A Judas

[Matthew 26–27; Mark 14; Luke 22;
John 13, and 18; Acts 1:18]

A traitor

Judas Iscariot, the betrayer of Jesus, has become the proverbial archetype of the traitor, a figure to be despised and feared. Shakespeare uses "worse than Judas" as a terrible insult in his *Richard II*, Act 3, Scene 2 (1597). Dante places Judas in the very lowest circle of Hell, condemned to lie head first in the Devil's mouth while his back is flayed by satanic talons.

Even the Bible takes a certain pleasure in telling how Judas came to a sticky end. In Matthew's famous account, he gives the thirty pieces of silver he has received as a fee for betraying Jesus back to the Pharisees, then hangs himself with a halter, like an animal. The Acts of the Apostles has a different story: The traitor used his ill-gotten gains to buy a field, then fell over and "burst asunder in the midst, and all his bowels gushed out."

Later writers were even more elaborate—Judas was said to have swelled up like a balloon, to have been covered in worms and running sores, or to have been "crushed by a chariot so that his bowels gushed out."

But not everyone has gone along with this savage view of the treacherous apostle. After all, as Jorge Luis Borges pointed out in a 1944 short story (*Three Versions of Judas*), the betrayal of Jesus was a crucial part of God's plan.

And Jesus only sacrificed his body to put that plan into effect—Judas had to sacrifice his soul.

Intriguingly, this belief may go back to the earliest days of Christianity. In the 1980s, a manuscript emerged that contained fragments from a long-lost "Gospel of Judas," which portrays him not as the villain of the New Testament, but as a hero, who is the only man to understand the true intentions of God.

Jumping Jehoshaphat

[1 Kings 15:24; 2 Chronicles 20:30–32]

A mild expletive signifying shock or surprise

The biblical Jehoshaphat is one of the lesser-known Jewish Kings, who ruled over the southern kingdom of Judah in the ninth century BC. He seems to have done a pretty good job as monarch, doing that "which was right in the sight of the Lord."

But it isn't his wisdom or justice which have made him famous. In fact, he owes his immortality to the lucky accident of having a name that sounds a lot like "Jesus."

The Ten Commandments forbid Christians from "taking the Lord's name in vain"—saying "Jesus" or "God" as an expletive counts as blasphemy. So, if an unfortunate "Je–" happens to slip out accidentally, one way to stay within the rules is to turn "Je–" into Jehoshaphat, in the same way that people these days sometimes say "oh fudge!"

"Jehosaphat" first appears as an exclamation in Samuel Hammet's 1857 novel *Sam Slick in Texas*, and it retains an "Old West" feel today, rarely used without the addition of a corny cowboy accent. As for why Jehoshaphat is so often "jumping," we can, alas, only speculate.

Kick Against the Pricks

[Acts 9:5]

**Rebel against authority, generally
without success**

This odd-sounding phrase comes from the story of St. Paul's conversion on the road to Damascus. Paul sees a blinding light and hears a voice crying: "I am Jesus whom thou persecutest. It is hard for thee to kick against the pricks."

The expression, which was an old proverb even in St. Paul's day, refers to the behavior of oxen who stubbornly resist the prodding of herdsmen's goads. By kicking against sharp cattle prods, all the ox achieves is to injure itself. Similarly, the idea is that, Paul hurts only himself by persecuting Jesus.

In modern usage, kicking against the pricks is generally regarded as a pretty bad idea. However, the spirit of self-destructive rebellion that the phrase captures has sometimes struck people as having a kind of glamour—in 1986, the saying was actually used as the title for an album by post-punk legends Nick Cave and the Bad Seeds.

Kiss of Death

[Matthew 26:48–50]

**Something—often well intentioned—which
condemns a person or project
to disaster and failure**

Matthew's Gospel tells how Judas Iscariot betrayed Jesus to the Jewish high priests, leading a crowd of thugs to arrest him in the Garden of Gethsemane. It was arranged that Judas would identify Jesus by greeting him with a kiss—this friendly gesture was the signal for the attackers to strike.

Two thousand years later, Mafia dons adopted the same trick, kissing people who were marked out for assassination. This idea of the "kiss of death" took root in the popular imagination of Prohibition America. In the early thirties, a Chicago woman called Margaret Collins actually had "The Kiss of Death" as a nickname, because of a gangland superstition that whomever she kissed would soon die.

In 1948 Lois Hunt Hardy—the "Kiss of Death Killer"—was sentenced to death for having distracted a man with a kiss so that her boyfriend could rob and kill him.

It's not just humans either. Scientists in 2002 found that the "kiss of death" was a tactic used by dinosaur ants. Ant queens would rub against rivals, marking them as targets for a horde of workers and soldiers: dinosaur ants are the world's largest, at over an inch long. Being kissed to death by one of them would be no joke.

Kiss of Life

[Matthew 26:48–50]

Mouth-to-mouth resuscitation; anything which revives or reinvigorates

"Kiss of life" is thought to have entered English as an opposite to Judas' treacherous "kiss of death" (see above). It's been used in Britain since at least 1961 as a term for mouth-to-mouth resuscitation, and its use in a more general sense goes back even further—in 1947 the phrase was briefly an advertising slogan for a firm of Detroit car salesmen.

Today, however, the kiss of life—both as a phrase and as an action—is falling out of favor. A 2007 study from Japan found that unconscious patients do better with chest compressions alone than they do when someone's trying to blow air down their throat.

And mouth-to-mouth resuscitation can go horribly wrong, with patients coughing up blood and vomiting and other such unpleasantness. In one famous incident from the 1970s, a British man almost died from a disease he caught when he gave the kiss of life to his dead pet parrot.

A Labor of Love

[1 Thessalonians 1:3; Hebrews 6:10]

A carefully tended project; something done out of enthusiasm rather than in hope of gain

This phrase comes from the First Epistle of St. Paul to the Thessalonians, which, written some time before AD 52, is probably the oldest book of the New Testament.

This message to the citizens of Thessalonica (in northern Greece) shows the strict apostle in unusually good spirits: "We give thanks to God always for you all," he writes kindly, "making mention of you in our prayers; remembering without ceasing your work of faith, and labor of love."

History does not record what exactly it was the Thessalonians were "laboring" at. Shakespeare, meanwhile, may have been echoing the biblical phrase with his 1598 comedy *Love's Labour's Lost*. One "labor of love" we can be certain of, however, is the 1983 album of that name by the reggae band UB40. Whether their efforts would have merited a friendly letter from St. Paul is another question.

A Lamb to the Slaughter

[Isaiah 53:7; Jeremiah 11:19; see also John 1:29]

**An innocent, being led unwittingly
towards disaster**

One of the Old Testament's most famous and discussed passages is Chapter 53 of the Book of Isaiah, which Christians believe is a prophecy about the life of Jesus. Isaiah describes the death of a mysterious "servant" of God: "He was oppressed, and he was afflicted, yet he opened not his mouth: he is brought as a lamb to the slaughter."

The lamb, as Christians like to point out, is a common metaphor for innocence in the Bible, and Jesus himself is sometimes called the Lamb of God (for example in John 1:29). Isaiah, they claim, is predicting the death of Christ, some five hundred years before the event.

Whether or not you credit Isaiah with prophetic powers, the phrase itself has enjoyed a long and varied afterlife as a poetic way to describe innocence led to destruction.

Chaucer uses the image in his *Man of Law's Tale* in 1386. In 1991, the horror film *The Silence of The Lambs* again uses the story of lambs screaming in a slaughterhouse to chilling effect.

And in 1953, Roald Dahl put his own particular twist on the tale with his short story *A Lamb to the Slaughter*. It tells of a wife who murders her husband using, rather imaginatively, a frozen leg of lamb which she then feeds to the policeman investigating the case.

The Land of Nod

[Genesis 4:16]

Sleep

Parents tucking their children in at night sometimes tell them to go to the Land of Nod. It's a cutesy way of telling someone to go to sleep, packing them off towards a world of pleasant dreams and fluffy fantasies.

But moms and dads might not be so fast to use the phrase if they knew its biblical origins. In Hebrew, the Land of Nod is the land of "exile" or "unrest," a cursed wilderness where the evil Cain is exiled after killing his brother Abel and where he lives out his miserable life as an outcast from God.

We owe our modern usage of the phrase to the eighteenth-century satirist Jonathan Swift, who used the

Land of Nod in *Gulliver's Travels* to mean the land of sleep because of a simple pun on "Nod" and "nodding off." His odd take on the biblical quote became firmly entrenched in the English language, so much so that there's even a village in Yorkshire that bears the phrase as its name.

A Leopard Can't Change His Spots

[Jeremiah 13:23]

It's impossible to change who you are

This rather exotic expression appears first in the Book of Jeremiah, one of the great prophets of the Old Testament. God is promising a full battery of plagues and misfortunes against a particularly sinful king and queen of Judah. And he warns them not to waste time trying to repent: "Can the Ethiopian change his skin, or the leopard his spots?" asks the Lord of Hosts rhetorically. Only then, he continues, "may ye also do good, that are accustomed to do evil."

The Romantic novelist Walter Scott was one of many writers to copy the phrase, in a context depressingly distant from what poor Jeremiah intended: "Let us put the Jew to ransom," he writes in his novel *Ivanhoe*, "since the leopard will not change his spots."

But there's an interesting twist to this tale: it turns out that leopards actually *do* change their spots. The spotty markings on a baby leopard's coat mutate over its lifetime into beautiful and complex rosettes.

Let He Who Is Without Sin Cast the First Stone

[John 8:7]

Don't be too quick to condemn others unless you're morally pure yourself

John's Gospel tells the story of a woman who was convicted of adultery and sentenced to death by stoning. The Pharisees, trying to catch Jesus out as always, like a gang of biblical Wile E. Coyotes, ask him what should be done with her.

It's a cunning dilemma. If Jesus tells them to stone her, he's playing the role of a judge, and can be reported to the Roman authorities. If he tells them to let her go, he's breaking the law as given to Moses, and can be accused of blasphemy.

And at first, it looks like Jesus is baffled. Instead of answering, he ignores them, doodling in the dust with his finger (it's the only time in the whole Bible that Jesus writes anything). At last, when they press him, he utters the famous line: "He that is without sin among you, let him first cast a stone at her."

The modern phrase, slightly polished up from the King James Version, gives a misleading idea of the nature of a biblical stoning. The victim wasn't pelted with pebbles. Instead, they were pushed violently off a high scaffold, before being crushed with a giant rock—a most unpleasant way to go.

Let Not the Sun Go Down on Your Wrath

[Ephesians 4:26]

Don't hold on to your anger for more than one day

This phrase is another piece of good advice from the letters of St. Paul, this time to the citizens of Ephesus. "Be ye angry, and sin not," advises the apostle. "Let not the sun go down upon your wrath."

This idea, that anger should be dealt with before sunset, was not, in fact, a new one to ancient thought. Pythagoras, a philosopher-mathematician who led a sort of classical hippy commune in southern Italy in the sixth century BC, also encouraged quarrelling followers "never to let the sun go down before they joined right hands, embraced each other, and were reconciled" (Plutarch, *Mora-lia*—On Brotherly Love).

At any rate, for Christians, not being wrathful was very sound policy. Anger, after all, is one of the famous Seven Deadly Sins, and the Italian poet Dante, in his *Inferno*, devotes a whole circle of Hell to this particular brand of sinner. The wrathful, he says, are condemned to stand forever in the River Styx, fighting each other or lurking, gurgling, beneath the inky waves.

Let There Be Light

[Genesis 1:3]

The words, according to Christians, that created the world

The opening four verses of the Bible are perhaps the most famous words in all world literature. As translated in the King James Version, they are also held up as one of the finest poetic accomplishments of all time:

> In the beginning God created the heaven and the earth.
> And the earth was without form, and void; and darkness was upon the face of the deep. And the Spirit of God moved upon the face of the waters.
> And God said, Let there be light: and there was light.
> And God saw the light, that it was good.

"Let there be light," also familiar in Latin as *fiat lux*, has become one of the most quoted Bible passages of all time. Schools and colleges all over the world have appropriated the divine command as their motto, using "light" as a metaphor for learning. The sci-fi author Isaac Asimov puts the words into the mouth (so to speak) of a giant world-creating super-computer in his 1956 short story, *The Last Question*.

Enterprising Web geeks have even translated the famous passage into LOLspeak—an invented dialect that exists only online: "At start," goes this bizarre version, "haz no lyte. An Ceiling Cat [God] says, "I can haz lyte?" An lyte wuz."

The late, great Alistair Cooke, a veteran radio journalist for the BBC, had his own version, imagining the *fiat lux* as spoken by a US government official: "The Supreme Being mandated the illumination of the Universe and this directive was enforced forthwith."

A Lions' Den

....

[Daniel 6:16]

A dangerous or difficult situation; a hostile environment

This phrase is a reference to the Book of Daniel, the great prophet of the Jewish exile in Babylon. The famous story is that he was accused by some jealous citizens of praying to God, in defiance of a recent imperial edict. "Then," says the Bible, "they brought Daniel, and cast him into the den of lions."

Daniel faced this fate with characteristic sangfroid, and when the "King" (the Persian Emperor Darius) came to check on him the next day, the prophet was standing quite calmly among the wild beasts, who had been pacified completely by a passing angel. Daniel's accusers were thrown into the den in his stead, along with their children and their wives, where the lions "brake all their bones in pieces," and that was the end of that.

In modern contexts, people who talk about going into a lions' den tend not to expect any angels to swoop in and save the day. The 2003 *Den of Lions*—a violent film about the Hungarian mafia—was decidedly unangelic. Artists going on stage at the Lion's Den Comedy Club in London have to face something more terrifying than any number of hungry predators—an audience.

Live by the Sword, Die by the Sword

[Matthew 26:52]

**People who make a career of violence
tend to die by violence**

The Gospel of Matthew tells how, when the Pharisees came to arrest Jesus, St. Peter (later to become the first Pope) "drew his sword, and struck a servant of the high priest's, and smote off his ear."

This uncharacteristic (and badly aimed) act of violence did not, of course, fit very well with the whole "turn the other cheek" ethos that Jesus was trying to promote. "Put up again thy sword into his place," said the angry Messiah. "For all they that take the sword shall perish with the sword."

People have been quoting this Bible passage ever since, as a way of discouraging violence, but the modern wording of the phrase only emerges in 1804, when the American diarist and statesman Gouverneur Morris misquotes it in his diary as "those who live by the sword shall perish by the sword."

In the twentieth century, "perish" gradually gave way to "die."

A Living Dog Is Better than a Dead Lion

[Ecclesiastes 9:4]

A solid achievement is worth more than hoped-for future gain

This odd phrase, from the Book of Ecclesiastes, was rare even in the nineteenth century. The Irish Romantic Thomas Moore made a living dog and a dead lion the subject of a comic poem in 1828, although he clearly prefers the deceased predator to the humdrum charms of man's best friend. A little-known writer called Stanley Weyman quoted the proverb in his 1902 adventure novel *In the King's Byways.*

From that modest peak, the phrase has now almost entirely disappeared from view—but there's a reason it deserves a mention. This ancient saying is one of the earliest expressions of a thought that remains popular and much quoted today, and which may have the lion and the dog as its earliest ancestor: "A bird in the hand is worth two in the bush."

Love Thy Neighbor

[Leviticus 19:18; Matthew 22:39; Galatians 5:14]

Treat others with care and respect as you would treat yourself

The Old Testament is full of injunctions about what one ought and oughtn't to do to one's neighbor. Don't covet "thy neighbor's ass," says Exodus. Don't "move a sickle unto thy neighbor's standing corn," says Deuteronomy. "Be not a witness against thy neighbor without cause," says the Book of Proverbs.

But by far the most important rule is summed up in one sentence of the Book of Leviticus: "Thou shalt not avenge, nor bear any grudge against the children of thy people, but thou shalt love thy neighbor as thyself."

This rule is a central statement in Christian ethics. In Matthew's Gospel, Jesus describes it as one of the two "great commandments" and in his Letter to the Galatians, St. Paul goes even further, saying that "the whole law is fulfilled" in that single principle.

Of course, a lot hinges on who exactly you think your neighbor is—a question that Jesus deals with in the parable of the Good Samaritan.

Man Does Not Live by Bread Alone

[Deuteronomy 8:3; Matthew 4:4]

Humans need spiritual as well as physical sustenance

In the Old Testament book of Deuteronomy Moses addresses the Israelites. God "humbled thee," he tells them, "and suffered thee to hunger . . . that he might make thee know that man doth not live by bread only but by every word that proceedeth out of the mouth of the Lord."

"Bread"—which, since it was the staple diet in the ancient Mediterranean, really means all food—is not enough for a human to live a full and happy life. Religious types have often taken this principle to the extreme, attempting to demonstrate that since man does not live by bread alone, he need not live on bread at all. Jesus, for example, famously did without food for forty days and forty nights during his temptation in the wilderness, quoting this phrase as his justification (Matthew 4:4).

Modern Christians are meant to fast during the forty days of Lent—a commemoration of Jesus' desert trials. However, despite two thousand years of trying, no one has been able to escape the fact that although bread isn't sufficient for life, it certainly helps. Today's Lenten fasts, therefore, tend to involve giving up chocolate or TV, rather than rejecting food entirely.

　　AMEN TO THAT!

A Man of Sorrows

[Isaiah 53:3]

Jesus; someone with many sufferings

The Book of Isaiah, in the Old Testament, speaks mysteriously of a "man of sorrows . . . acquainted with grief" who was "wounded for our transgressions . . . the chastisement of our peace was upon him." From the description it sounds uncannily like a reference to Jesus, despite having been written some five hundred years before he was even born.

Medieval readers didn't doubt for a second that this was genuine prophecy in action, and the image of Christ as the Man of Sorrows—wearing his crown of thorns and dripping blood from the sacred wounds—became one of the defining images for religious painters of the early Renaissance. Pallid, sorrowful faces can be seen these days peering down from the walls of half the museums in Europe.

Jesus is often still called the Man of Sorrows today, although the expression can be used to describe anyone who's in a really bad way. The *Baltimore Morning Herald* was using the phrase to describe an Austrian emperor as long ago as 1898. Other famous recipients of this unlikely epithet include Abraham Lincoln and, oddly, the humorist Mark Twain.

Man Proposes but God Disposes

[Proverbs 16:9]

Don't count on things going according to plan

This little-known phrase has a roundabout history that traces back to the Book of Proverbs, which tells us: "A man's heart deviseth his way but the Lord directeth his steps."

The meaning is clear but, as proverbs go, it's hardly catchy. In 1418, Thomas à Kempis, in his *De Imitatione Christi*, attempted an upgrade with the Latin: *Homo proponit, sed Deus disponit*. This jingle, translated straightforwardly into English, is the source of the modern wording.

The best poetic expression of this same thought, however, comes in Robbie Burns's *To a Mouse* (1786):

> The best laid schemes o' mice an' men
> Gang aft a-gley,
> An' lea'e us nought but grief an' pain,
> For promised joy.

This colorful Scottish version is much more familiar than the English rhyme.

Manna from Heaven

[Exodus 16:12–16]

A godsend

After escaping from Egypt in the Book of Exodus, the Israelites find themselves wandering in the Sinai Desert, hungry, tired and far from the Promised Land. To keep them going, God creates a miraculous food called manna, which they find each morning scattered "upon the face of the wilderness."

In modern usage, "manna from heaven" can be applied to anything which appears out of nowhere to solve a serious problem. But although it's a familiar phrase, no one can agree what the original manna actually was. Candidates include resin from tamarisk trees, "honeydew" from the intestines of insects, dried lichen or even magic mushrooms. Even the ancient Israelites seem to have been confused. One account of the origin of the word "manna" is the supposed ancient Hebrew *man hu*—"what is it?"

Liverpudlian slang offers another suggestion. The 1966 publication *ABZ of Scouse* has the phrase "Manna from hevving"—meaning "bird droppings."

A Martyr

[Acts 20:22; Revelation 2:13]

**Someone who dies for a cause; someone who
suffers greatly (or pretends to)**

Strictly speaking, "martyr," from the Greek *martus*, should
just mean witness. The New Testament commonly talks
about Christians as "martyrs" for Jesus, meaning only
that they bear witness to his teachings.

It was St. Stephen who, around AD 34, first began to
give the word its special meaning when his habit of "witnessing" Christianity landed him in trouble with the high
priests in Jerusalem. Stephen was stoned to death, and
when the Book of Acts calls him a *martus*, the King James
Bible renders the word as "martyr" instead of "witness"—
from Stephen onwards, "witnessing" and death would be
inextricably linked.

Stephen was the first of many. A 2001 report on the
annual Christian "megacensus" claims that as many as
seventy million martyrs have died for Christianity since
AD 30, including more than ten thousand crucified, more
than a hundred thousand savaged by wild dogs, and several hundred either thrown from aircraft, run over by
tanks or even eaten by piranhas.

In modern usage, the word has broadened out beyond
its Christian roots. Shakespeare introduced the idea of being a martyr to love in 1600 with *Henry IV Part 2*, and

these days you can be a martyr to pretty much anything, from science to marriage to even rheumatism.

A Nest of Vipers

....

[Matthew 3:7]

A group of traitors or evil people

The use of snakes as a metaphor for evildoers comes up repeatedly in the Gospels. The unfortunate reptiles did, after all, have some severe image problems after the whole Garden of Eden/Forbidden Fruit scandal. Jesus himself breaks with his customary mildness to hurl this particular term of abuse at various scribes and Pharisees who manage to get on his holy nerves.

It is John the Baptist, however, who first uses the expression, when a group of unwelcome holy men turn up at the River Jordan hoping for his blessing. "O generation of vipers," shouts the saint. "Who hath warned you to flee from the wrath to come?"

Although the original Greek *gennemata echidnon* could easily be translated "nest of vipers," the wording of the modern phrase is not documented in English until it appears as the title of a pamphlet in 1644, which described an array of "treasonous plotters" as "a nest of the vilest vipers that ever Africk or Nile did produce."

No Room at the Inn

....

[Luke 2:7]

No space to accommodate visitors

In a scene familiar from any school Nativity play, Joseph and Mary arrive in the town of Bethlehem where they have been summoned by the Roman authorities to complete a census and register for tax. But although Mary is heavily pregnant, the town is so full of people on the same errand that there is "no room for them in the inn." Instead, they sleep in a stable and it is there that Jesus is finally born, with a manger for his bed.

"No room at the inn" has been used as an expression ever since, usually when encouraging people not to shut their doors to those in need. The current Archbishop of York, John Sentamu, for example, compared Joseph and Mary to modern-day asylum-seekers needing shelter. Writing in 2000, conservative commentator Lew Rockwell drew a different lesson from the phrase: If there was no room at the inn, he wrote, it was because of a market distortion created by the Roman emperor's lamentable devotion to the economics of tax and spend.

No Rest for the Wicked

[Isaiah 57:20-21 and 48:22]

Gotta keep working

According to the Book of Isaiah: "The wicked are like the troubled sea when it cannot rest, whose waters cast up mire and dirt. There is no peace, saith my God, to the wicked."

Since at least the sixteenth century, the phrase "no peace for the wicked" has been used as a dire warning to the unrighteous about the penalties of sin. From the nineteenth century, the misquotation "no rest for the wicked" begins to appear, although it has the same stern sense.

But in an odd shift of meaning (first recorded in an issue of *Harper's Magazine* in 1869), the quote can now be used in a jocular, ironic way, where the "wicked" person who is allowed no rest is in fact the person who says the phrase. Said in the same rueful way that we sometimes say "for my sins," it acknowledges that human life is full of hard work and that one just has to get on with it.

This usage enjoyed a major boost in popularity when "no rest for the wicked" appeared as a title for the popular US cartoon strip *Little Orphan Annie* in 1933. In 1988, however, rock legend and celebrity bat-eater Ozzy Osbourne used the phrase as the title for his fifth studio album, restoring to the words their proper measure of Old Testament severity and gloom.

Nothing New Under the Sun

[Ecclesiastes 1:9]

**Everything that happens has happened before;
plus ça change, plus c'est la même chose**

"What profit hath a man of all his labor?" asks the Book of Ecclesiastes gloomily. "The thing that hath been, it is that which shall be; and that which is done is that which shall be done: and there is no new thing under the sun."

This uncharacteristic attack of Eeyoreishness from the Bible has caused problems for later commentators. After all, there have been one or two new things under the sun since the middle of the first millennium BC.

The eighteenth-century scholar John Gill claimed valiantly that the various new inventions of his age had probably been tried already by the ancient Chinese, or by other forgotten civilizations. Whether he would have used the same excuse for spaceships and supercomputers will sadly remain forever unknown.

As Old as Methuselah

[Genesis 5:21–29; see also Job 15:2–9]

Very old

When Jeanne Calment died in France at the grand old age of 122, her friends thought she'd had a good run for her money. According to the *Guinness Book of Records*, she lived longer than any human since records began. But if you'd said she was as old as Methuselah then strictly speaking you would have been totally wrong.

At the age of 122, Methuselah—the grandfather of Noah—was just getting started. According to the Book of Genesis, he had his first child when he was 187 and kept on "begetting" sons and daughters for another seven centuries. By the time he died, he had been alive for 969 years.

As the oldest man in the Bible, Methuselah has become a proverbial comparison for anyone who lives to an extreme old age. He also, oddly, gave his name to a type of bottle: a Methuselah of wine holds as much as eight ordinary wine bottles—perhaps appropriate, considering he lived nearly eight times as long as the world's oldest woman.

Out of the Mouths of Babes

[Psalms 8:2; Matthew 21:16]

**Children can say clever or important things;
a traditional exclamation for when someone
displays wisdom beyond their years**

The idea that it's sometimes children who are wisest runs deep in human thought. As in the case of the Emperor's New Clothes, it sometimes takes the honest, unjaded voice of youth to tell us what we *should* already know—that the mighty monarch is prancing around in the nude.

In the Bible, this idea comes up in the Book of Psalms: "Out of the mouth of babes and sucklings hast thou [God] ordained strength." In Matthew's Gospel, Jesus actually misquotes the expression: "Have ye never read, Out of the mouth of babes and sucklings thou hast perfected praise?" Jesus' version is based on a Greek translation of the Old Testament called the Septuagint, rather than the Hebrew original.

In modern speech, the quote has become a familiar saying, which usually, but not always, expresses admiration for some precocious childish utterance. In 2002 however, the New York *Daily News* put a new spin on the expression for an article about profanity in young children. "From the mouths of babes," thundered the headline, "comes forth a stream of foul language."

A Peace Offering

[Leviticus 3; see also Genesis 22]

A gift to defuse an argument

These days a peace offering is usually nothing more than a bunch of flowers from a guilty husband, and perhaps a gushing card. But the Israelites in biblical times took these things much more seriously. For them, the only proper offering was a full-on animal sacrifice.

Leviticus describes the proper procedure: "If his oblation be a sacrifice of peace offering . . . he shall offer it without blemish before the Lord . . . kill it at the door of the tabernacle . . . and Aaron's sons the priests shall sprinkle the blood upon the altar round about." The fat, kidneys and liver were burned on a fire, and the smoke was thought to rise up to Heaven to please God.

This sacrificial custom was common among ancient Near Eastern civilizations and, as with other cultures, there are intriguing hints that the earliest sacrifices may in fact have been human. Part of the sacrificial ritual, for example, involved the dedicator placing his hand on the animal, to symbolize the fact that the unfortunate creature was standing in his stead.

This act of symbolic substitution (some would call it cheating) is most famously evoked in the story of Abraham and Isaac, in which the patriarch is asked to sacrifice his only son as an offering to God. It is only at the last minute that Isaac is rescued by an angel, his place being taken by a nearby ram.

Abraham and Isaac

It's hard to think of anything more unpleasant than being ordered to kill your own child. But when God tells Abraham to sacrifice his beloved son Isaac on a nearby mountain, the gutsy patriarch doesn't bat an eyelid. Instead, he and the boy set off the very next morning, as if on a father–son camping trip.

It's only once they arrive at the place of the sacrifice that Isaac begins to suspect that something's up. "Behold the fire and the wood," he says to his father, "but where is the lamb for a burnt offering?"

Too late. Soon, Isaac is bound and on the altar and it's only when Abraham is about to plunge the knife into the boy's heart that an angel appears like a host on a candid camera show and stays his hand. In reward for his exceptional devotion, Abraham becomes the great ancestor of the people of Israel.

A Philistine

[Genesis 21:32; Judges 13:1; and elsewhere]

A boorish person; someone with no appreciation of culture or art

The historical Philistines were one of several mysterious tribes to arrive in the southern Mediterranean around the end of the second millennium BC. They first appear in ancient Egyptian records in 1180 BC, and quickly became settled in a coastal strip roughly in the area of modern Gaza.

In the Bible, the Philistines were the perennial enemies of the kings of Israel, engaging them in a string of battles before finally being subdued by King David. In the eighth century BC, the Philistines, like the Israelites, were conquered by the Assyrian Empire and disappeared as a distinct cultural group, although their name survives in the modern word "Palestine."

The current meaning of Philistine, however, comes not from the Bible but from the Universities of Germany, where the students—"sons of academic Israel," as the nineteenth-century traveler John Russell put it—sniffily referred to the non-academic townsfolk as "philistines." The word had spread to Britain by 1825, to describe anyone judged to have an insufficient appreciation of learning and the arts.

Physician, Heal Thyself

[Luke 4:23]

Look after your own problems before interfering with mine

Luke's Gospel records an episode in which Jesus visits his childhood village of Nazareth. News of his divine cures has spread by now, and he expects that the Nazarenes will tell him: "Physician, heal thyself"—cure problems at home (i.e. in Nazareth) before trying to help other people.

In modern English, the phrase is a straightforward biblical reference. Interestingly, though, it is quoted by Jesus as an expression that is already in general use. Clearly this was a common saying in ancient Israel, a part of everyday Judaean speech that has been preserved through the millennia just because Jesus happened to mention it to his disciples.

At any rate, in the ancient world, telling a physician to go away and "heal" himself was a pretty good idea. The science of medicine has advanced so slowly that, according to some estimates, doctors were more likely to kill you than cure you until as recently as the discovery of penicillin in 1928.

The Powers That Be

[Romans 13:1, 2]

The authorities—often in a resigned or ironic sense

"Let every soul be subject unto the higher powers. . ." says St. Paul in his Letter to the Romans. "The powers that be are ordained of God. Whosoever therefore resisteth the power, resisteth the ordinance of God."

For writers like the seventeenth-century philosopher James Tyrrell, this was an instruction to be taken seriously. "The Powers that be, that is, the Princes and Emperors who now govern the World, are ordained and appointed by God," he says earnestly in his 1694 *Bibliotheca Politica*, "and that thus it is God himself tells us."

"The powers that be" became a common shorthand for any figures of "divinely ordained" authority, but as political thought developed, and the "divine right" of kings to rule (as believed in by, for example, Charles I) fell out of fashion, the phrase acquired an ironic edge. When Rudyard Kipling wrote in his poem "Study of an Elevation, in Indian Ink" (1886) that

> Potiphar Gubbins, C.E.,
> Is dear to the Powers that Be,

he *didn't* mean it as a compliment, and in modern usage, that sense persists: "the powers that be" generally means "The powers that exist—but I wish they didn't."

A Prodigal Son

[Luke 15:11-32]

**Someone who has been away for too long but
has finally returned**

"Prodigal" is a rare English word which originally meant "reckless" or "extravagant." These days, however, it's most often used to mean something like "wayward" or "wandering," a shift in sense that comes from the parable of the prodigal son.

Luke's Gospel tells of a farmer who had two sons. One day the youngest son sets off into the world to make his fortune.

But instead of making a fortune, this "prodigal" son squanders one, spending his father's money on fine wine, fancy clothes and exotic women like a sort of biblical trust fund kid. Before long he's burned through every penny, and is reduced to herding pigs, an unutterably demeaning profession for a Jew.

Soon, in a scene that's probably been replayed by thousands of teenagers over the millennia, the repentant son turns up penniless back at his father's door. Naturally, he expects the worst but as soon as his father sees him, he gives orders for a feast of celebration: "Bring hither the fatted calf and kill it; and let us eat and be merry. For this my son was dead, and is alive again; he was lost, and is found."

The moral of this "fatted calf" feast is that God loves a repentant sinner—something that has always struck life's *non*-prodigal sons as terribly unfair.

Put Away Childish Things

[1 Corinthians 13:11]

To grow up, or get serious

This expression comes from an often-quoted passage of St. Paul's First Letter to the Corinthians. "When I was a child," he writes, "I spake as a child, I understood as a child, I thought as a child: but when I became a man, I put away childish things."

The idea is that just as children gain a whole new level of understanding when they grow up, so humans will gain a new level of understanding when they get to Heaven. In modern use, however, the phrase usually has a more literal meaning—it's time to grow up and get a grip.

The quote has always been popular, but in 2009 it got a new lease of life when Barack Obama used it in his inaugural address. "We Americans," said the president, "remain a young nation, but in the words of Scripture, the time has come to set aside childish things . . . to choose our better history."

Whether US politics has lived up to that lofty vision since then is—one might say—debatable.

Put Words in Someone's Mouth

[Isaiah 51:16]

To misrepresent what someone has said

In the Book of Isaiah, God says: "I have put my words in thy mouth." He's talking about religion—his words, put into the mouths of priests and prophets. It's a common idea in ancient thought. Ancient poets like Homer and Virgil openly declared that their art was produced by some god, working through them.

But in a religious context, the idea that certain utterances are literally the word of God has some odd consequences. Those Christians, for example, who believe that the Bible is the perfect and complete word of God occasionally have to do some impressive mental contortionism to accommodate apparent contradictions. Catholics at the First Vatican Council of 1870 went even further by claiming that the Pope, as God's mouthpiece on earth, literally cannot be wrong (at least when he's speaking in an official capacity)—a belief that was used to good comic effect in Kevin Smith's 1999 comedy *Dogma*.

Of course, in modern English, putting words into someone's mouth is generally considered a bad thing. It's often used as part of the rhetorical "straw man" technique, when you misrepresent your opponent's beliefs (setting up a straw man) before knocking them down.

Quote Chapter and Verse

**To cite the precise authority for something;
to know a source perfectly**

No book in history is so often quoted as the Bible and it quickly became clear that the world needed a system for identifying where in the many different books each quote had come from. It was Jewish scholars in the sixth to tenth centuries AD who invented the structure of the Bible as we know it, where each book was divided into numbered chapters and each chapter into numbered verses.

Christians were a little slower. The New Testament was given chapters by Archbishop Langton only in the thirteenth century, and verses weren't added until the Geneva Bible edition of 1557.

In an age when the Bible was regarded as an unquestionable moral authority, being able to quote chapter and verse was a major advantage, and one which people spent a lot of time cultivating. It might seem like an implausible achievement today, but the early Quaker George Fox (1624–91) was said to be able to recite the entire Bible by heart, chapters, verses and all.

These days, the phrase has broadened out to include knowledge of any authority, not just the Bible.

Reap the Whirlwind

[Hosea 8:7]

**Bear the negative consequences
of one's actions**

Hosea, one of the more doom-laden prophets of the Old Testament, had this to say about the Israelites: "They have sown the wind and they shall reap the whirlwind . . . Israel is swallowed up."

The "wind" is folly and frivolity (compare "windbag" today). The "whirlwind," by contrast, is utter destruction, which will consume the land of Israel.

The most famous modern use of the phrase was by Sir Arthur "Bomber" Harris, in the Second World War. At the outset of Britain's area bombing campaign against German cities, he quoted Hosea: "The Nazis entered this war under the rather childish delusion that they were going to bomb everyone else, and nobody was going to bomb them . . . They sowed the wind, and now they are going to reap the whirlwind."

You Reap What You Sow

[Galatians 6:7–9]

Bad behavior will come back to haunt you

"Whatsoever a man soweth," writes St. Paul in his Letter to the Galatians, "that shall he also reap." It's a fundamental principle of justice that those who do ill will suffer the consequences, whether through karma, the law or the wrath of God.

The problem is that the world is full of bad people who are visibly *not* suffering at all. The TV series *Mad Men* put this well: "How do you sleep at night?" one character asks. "On a bed made of money," says the other.

But that hasn't stopped the phrase becoming popular today. The saying even achieved musical success when Lou Reed used St. Paul's words as a haunting outro in his 1972 song, "Perfect Day."

Red Sky at Night, Shepherds' Delight. Red Sky in Morning, Shepherds' Warning

[Matthew 16:2,3]

An ancient axiom for weather forecasting:
Red skies in the evening are a sign of fair weather;
red skies in the morning are a sign of coming rain

This famous rhyme is one of the most ancient scientific maxims ever recorded. Jesus, in the Gospel of Matthew, repeats the proverb in passing while arguing with a group of holy men: "When it is evening, ye say, 'It will be fair weather: for the sky is red.' And in the morning: 'It will be foul weather to day, for the sky is red and lowring.' "

The "shepherds" of today's version are a medieval addition, probably a hangover from the time when England's wealth was largely based on the profitable wool trade. Shakespeare, in his 1593 poem *Venus and Adonis*, is the first written source for the link:

> Like a red morn that ever yet betokened,
> Wreck to the seaman, tempest to the field,
> Sorrow to the shepherds, woe unto the birds,
> Gusts and foul flaws to herdmen and to herds.

The modern wording of the phrase probably evolved during the nineteenth century, appearing as "an old rhyme" in a New Zealand newspaper from 1884, and in an issue of *Punch* magazine in 1920.

Interestingly, this ancient adage actually has some basis in scientific fact. Red skies are often caused by low sunlight reflecting back off clouds. In the evening, those clouds will be in the east, opposite the setting sun, whereas the sky to the west will be clear. That means, since weather systems generally pass from west to east, that the clouds have blown over and fine weather is on the way.

To Be Someone's Rock

[Deuteronomy 32:37; Matthew 7:24–27 and 16:18]

To be a reliable supporter or foundation for someone; a source of comfort and inner strength

The rock as a metaphor for a firm spiritual foundation is an old one in the Bible. It appears as early as Deuteronomy, when the false gods of heathens are described as "their rock in whom they trusted." In the Gospels, Jesus extends the metaphor with his famous parable of the man who builds his house upon a rock.

But the most famous "rock" of all is the Apostle Simon. In Matthew's Gospel, Jesus grandly rechristens him. "Thou art Peter," he says, "and upon this rock I will build my church."

In ancient Greek, this abrupt name change makes rather more sense. Jesus was punning: the name Peter is simply the Greek word *petros*, meaning rock.

St. Peter (or St. Rock—as we might call him) became the first Pope of the Catholic Church, and the "rock" metaphor became entrenched in the English language.

The Root of All Evil

....

[1 Timothy 6:10]

Money, or the love of money

St. Paul offers the following thought in his First Epistle to Timothy: "The love of money is the root of all evil . . . [those who covet it] have erred from the faith, and pierced themselves through with many sorrows."

Often misquoted as "money is the root of all evil," the phrase can refer either to money or to greed, one of the Seven Deadly Sins. The "many sorrows" with which the greedy are pierced take graphic form in Dante's *Inferno*, where the greedy and the avaricious joust eternally, pushing heavy weapons with their bare chests.

Richard Dawkins, champion of militant secularism, also used the phrase two thousand years later as the title for his 2006 documentary series arguing against the existence of God. For him, however, this "root of all evil" was not money or greed, but religion itself.

The Salt of the Earth

....

[Matthew 5:13]

Virtuous, honest or reliable people

In Matthew's Gospel, Jesus addresses a crowd of the faithful and his assembled disciples: "Ye are the salt of the earth," he says. "But if the salt have lost his savor, wherewith shall it be salted? It is thenceforth good for nothing, but to be cast out, and to be trodden under foot of men."

At first sight, it's a rather odd expression. But in its ancient context, it makes rather more sense. Salt was not only very valuable (it is the origin of the word "salary") but also, in the hot climate of Judaea, was an important preservative for food, preventing it from going bad. In the same way, the disciples and apostles were charged with preserving the world from evil and fending off corruption.

And the use of unsalted food as a metaphor for things that are morally bad has deep roots in our language. After all, we often describe shifty or evil-looking people as "unsavory."

To Have the Scales Fall from One's Eyes

[Acts 9:18]

Suddenly to see clearly or perceive the truth about something

This strange expression is a reference to the conversion of St. Paul, who was struck blind by God on the way to persecute the Christians of Damascus. The Book of Acts tells us how Jesus, who was nearby, dispatched one of his followers to heal the afflicted oppressor: "Immediately there fell from his eyes as it had been scales, and he received sight forthwith, and arose, and was baptized."

The meaning, not very clear in the King James translation, is that it was *as if* scales (the original Greek word can also mean "snowflakes" or "eggshells") had fallen from Paul's eyes.

Today, the phrase generally implies a sudden moment of clarity after a long period of deception, as captured in Neil Munro's 1898 short story collection *The Lost Pibroch:* "One may look at a person for years and not see the reality till a scale falls from the eyes."

A Scapegoat

[Leviticus 16:8]

**Someone who is unfairly made to take the
blame for something**

The Book of Leviticus describes the proper ceremonies to be observed on the Jewish Day of Atonement, when the land of Israel would be ritually cleansed of its sins. The procedure was that one goat would be offered to God as a sacrifice, while the other—the "scapegoat"—would be symbolically loaded with all the misdeeds of the nation before being driven into the wilderness.

This ceremony was said to have been carried out each year since the Exodus from Egypt. It did, however, acquire one important modification after an unfortunate incident in which the scapegoat wandered out of the wilderness and merrily back towards Jerusalem. To prevent a repeat of this extremely bad omen, subsequent priests arranged that the scapegoat's journey to the wilderness should start with a headlong plunge down a local cliff. After that, scapegoats became significantly less mobile.

Separate the Sheep from the Goats

[Matthew 25:31–46 and 3:12; John 10:1–17]

To distinguish the worthy from the unworthy

A common metaphor in the Gospels has Jesus as the "good shepherd" who "giveth his life for the sheep." Indeed, the word *pastor* is simply "shepherd" in Latin. But although he is devoted to his sheep, other quadrupeds aren't so lucky. "When the Son of Man shall come in glory," says Matthew's Gospel, "he shall set the sheep on his right hand, but the goats on the left." The sheep go to Jesus to receive eternal life but the goats (which were less valuable as livestock) "shall go away into everlasting punishment."

There's a Serpent in Every Paradise

[Genesis 3:1–5]

Nothing is ever perfect

Of all the animals, the unfortunate serpent has been cursed with the worst possible reputation. It has been a symbol of treachery and poisonous intent since the time of Chaucer, who wrote in his *Summoner's Tale* (*c.* 1405) of "the serpent that so slyly creepeth . . . and stingeth subtly."

In Shakespeare, the "serpent's tongue" is the ultimate emblem of deceit (we still sometimes say that liars speak with "forked tongues"). In modern usage, the "serpent" in "every paradise" stands for the inevitable flaw that pollutes even the most pleasant surroundings.

The source of all this bad press is the Book of Genesis, in which the first serpent, who was "more subtil than any beast of the field," tempts Eve to eat the forbidden fruit. When God finds out, he is most displeased: "Because thou hast done this," he says wrathfully, "thou art cursed; upon thy belly shalt thou go, and dust shalt thou eat all the days of thy life."

Intriguingly, this serpent of Genesis appears not to have moved on its belly until *after* God's curse, implying perhaps that creation's first snakes may have had legs—or at least that they were very good at bouncing on their tails. The other odd detail is that nowhere in Genesis does it say that this serpent was in fact Satan, or any other kind of devil. The idea that it was Satan who tempted Adam and Eve doesn't appear until the non-canonical Wisdom of Solomon, written hundreds of years later.

Set One's House in Order

[Isaiah 38:1]

To sort oneself out

Chapter 38 of the Book of Isaiah tells the story of Hezekiah, King of Judah, who was "sick unto death." God, through Isaiah, gives Hezekiah a rather blunt message: "Set thine house in order: for thou shalt die, and not live."

This wasn't an instruction to tidy the living room. By "house" the King James translators mean "household"—the king is being told to urgently sort out his will and his succession.

In this general sense, the phrase remains popular in English today. For political journalists, it's been (some would say literally) a godsend: if you ever need a pun for a headline on squabbles in the Houses of Parliament or Congress, this is one phrase you can count on.

Set Someone's Teeth
on Edge

[Jeremiah 31:29–30; Ezekiel 18:2]

To make someone wince; to irritate someone

In the Bible, this phrase refers to a literal sensation, an uncomfortable feeling in the teeth caused by eating something sour. It also forms part of an ancient Babylonian proverb, as found in the Book of Jeremiah: "The fathers have eaten a sour grape, and the children's teeth are set on edge." The meaning is that children are punished for their fathers' crimes.

It is Shakespeare who popularized the expression in modern English, however, using it in his play *Henry IV Part I* to describe the effect of listening to bad poetry:

> I had rather hear a brazen canstick turn'd,
> Or a dry wheel grate on the axle-tree;
> And that would set my teeth nothing on edge,
> Nothing so much as mincing poetry:
> 'Tis like the forced gait of a shuffling nag.
> Act 3, Scene 1

Seven Deadly Sins

[Proverbs 6:16–19; Galatians 5:19–21; Mark 7:21–22]

The seven main sins in Christianity: pride, wrath, envy, lust, gluttony, avarice and sloth

The idea of listing sins goes back in the Bible as far as the Book of Proverbs, which says that seven things "are an abomination" to the Lord. However, the list, which includes things like "a proud look" or "a lying tongue," doesn't look much like the one we know today.

New Testament lists like the one found in Mark are more familiar, though much longer.

In fact, the modern list only emerges from theological thought in the Middle Ages, before being made famous in Dante's *Inferno* in the fourteenth century. He assigns each of the sins to one of the seven circles of Hell, with punishments appropriate to the crime.

The deadly sins made a fresh impact on modern culture when director David Fincher used them as a basis for his 1995 horror film *Seven*, in which "sinners" are murdered according to their sin. In the disgusting opening scene, for example, detectives find the body of a gluttonous man who has been forced to eat himself to death.

A Sign of the Times

[Matthew 16:3]

**An indicator of current trends—generally
trends of which the speaker disapproves**

Beloved of grumpy old men everywhere, this phrase is commonly used to pick out something that exemplifies what's wrong with society today.

These "signs" tend not to be very earth-shattering. Instead, the targets are often cases where political correctness or modern sensibilities are judged to have gone over the top—a professor insisting that the word "pet" is demeaning to animals, to take a recent example, or a woman live-blogging her birth pangs on Twitter.

To hear people talk about such small foolishnesses, you'd think the world was about to end. Of course, when the phrase was first used, in Matthew's Gospel, that was precisely the idea. "O ye hypocrites," says Jesus to a group of long-suffering Pharisees. "Ye can discern the face of the sky; but can ye not discern the signs of the times?" It's not just any old "times" he's talking about. Rather, he is berating them on their failure to recognize the coming of the Messiah and, therefore, the coming apocalypse.

A Slaughter of the Innocents

[Matthew 2:1–16]

A massacre or infanticide

Matthew's Gospel tells how the wise men—acting rather less wisely than usual—stopped to visit King Herod on the way to Bethlehem to worship the baby Jesus. Of course, when they told him they were off to see the future "King of the Jews," Herod was most displeased. Indeed, he was "exceeding wroth" and, in an attempt to forestall this presumed usurper, "sent forth, and slew all the children that were in Bethlehem, and in all the coasts thereof, from two years old and under."

Fortunately, Jesus, Mary and Joseph had escaped to Egypt, having been tipped off by an angel, but the rest of Bethlehem's children weren't so lucky. Medieval writers claimed that there were as many as 144,000 of these "Holy Innocents"—sometimes called the first Christian martyrs.

This massacre made a deep impression on later culture. The Holy Innocents have their own feast day, their own carol (the famous Coventry Carol of 1534) and have inspired an endless quantity of gory Renaissance art. Even modern creative types can't stay away from the theme. A thriller called *Slaughter of the Innocents* came out to modest acclaim in 1993, and the story even comes up as a plot-line in the latest sequel to Paramount's *Kung Fu Panda*.

Sod's Law

The imaginary law that states that whatever can go wrong usually does

Sod's law has been described as an "unshakeable law" of human existence. A 1970 issue of *New Statesman* magazine, one of the earliest occurrences of the phrase, describes it as a "force in nature which causes it to rain mostly at weekends, which makes you get flu when you are on holiday, and which makes the phone ring just as you've got into the bath."

But who was Sod, and why is his name attached to such a bleak rule? The trail leads back to the nineteenth century when the word "sod" emerged as vulgar slang, defined in G. W. Matsell's *Rogue's Lexicon* (1859) as "a worn-out debauchee, whom excess of indulgence has rendered unnatural."

"Sod" was short for "sodomite"—an inhabitant of the city of Sodom. The biblical Sodomites were destroyed by God for "giving themselves over to fornication, and going after strange flesh." For later Christians, "strange flesh" could mean only one thing: the sodomites were homo-sexuals. "Sod," in un-PC Victorian England, therefore became an all-purpose term of casual abuse. It is more commonly referred to as Murphy's law in the US.

Lot and the Angels

When God tells Abraham that he intends to destroy the cities of Sodom and Gomorrah, Abraham pleads with him to change his mind for the sake of any righteous souls that might be living there. So God decides to investigate, sending a pair of undercover angels to see whether there really are any good men in Sodom.

As it turns out, there's one. This is Lot, who receives the angels hospitably, even without realizing their divine origins, and defends them when an angry mob gathers outside his door. "Behold now," Lot tells the crowd. "I have two daughters which have not known man; let me, I pray you, bring them out unto you, and do ye to them as is good in your eyes; only unto these men do nothing."

Luckily, the angels do some well-timed smiting before Lot can make good his offer, and the next morning Lot, his daughters and his wife leave town for good.

A Soft Answer Turns Away Wrath

[Proverbs 15:1]

A gentle response will often defuse
a tense situation

This nugget of advice comes from the Book of Proverbs, said to have been written by King Solomon himself. "A soft answer turneth away wrath," writes the wise monarch, "but grievous words stir up anger."

This biblical maxim has been popular ever since. Even more popular, however, is President Teddy Roosevelt's famous twist on the same idea, invented for a speech in 1901. The secret of successful foreign policy, he said, is to "speak softly," but "carry a big stick."

The Straight and Narrow

[Matthew 7:13–14]

The path of virtue, that leads to salvation

"Wide is the gate, and broad is the way," says Jesus in the Sermon on the Mount, "that leadeth to destruction, and many there be which go in thereat." On the other hand: "Strait is the gate, and narrow is the way, which leadeth unto life, and few there be that find it."

These days the phrase almost always uses the spelling "straight" rather than "strait." Strictly speaking, this is a mistake. "Strait" isn't an old-fashioned form of "straight," it's a completely different word, meaning not "direct" (as in "go straight there") but narrow (as in Straits of Gibraltar).

The misspelling comes from a popular 1842 hymn from *Hymns and Scenes of Childhood* by Jane Leeson, which also introduces the familiar modern wording:

> Suffer not my steps to stray
> From the straight and narrow way.

This Bible passage is also the source of the expression "the primrose path." In his tragedy *Hamlet*, Shakespeare has Ophelia contrast the strait and narrow path to heaven with the broad path to destruction:

Do not, as some ungracious pastors do,
Show me the steep and thorny way to heaven;
Whiles, like a puff'd and reckless libertine,
Himself the primrose path of dalliance treads
Act 1, Scene 3

The Sin of Onan

....

[Genesis 38:8–10]

A euphemistic term for masturbation

Onan is a minor character from the Book of Genesis, one of the sons of Judah and grandson of the Israelite patriarch Jacob. Onan's brother died leaving a widow, but no children. Onan was then expected, in accordance with ancient law, to fulfill his brother's conjugal duties.

Onan, reasonably enough, was uncomfortable with this arrangement. "Onan knew that the seed should not be his, and it came to pass, when he went in unto his brother's wife, that he spilled [his seed] on the ground."

God killed the unfortunate Onan for his impiety, and his name was banished into obscurity until 1715, when an anonymous pamphlet about the dangers of masturbation coined the word *Onania* for its euphemistic title. The subtitle clarified that "onania" was "the heinous sin of self-pollution"—an "abominable practice" with "frightful consequences" including impotence, consumption, epilepsy and scrawny calves (see Jean Stengers and Anne van Neck, *Masturbation*).

The name of Onan has been synonymous with solitary seed-spilling ("seed," or in Latin—*semen*) ever since.

The Spirit Is Willing, but the Flesh Is Weak

....

[Matthew 26:36–45]

Intending to act morally is easy, but turning thoughts into deeds is much harder

After the last supper, Jesus retires to the Garden of Gethsemane to await his arrest and eventual crucifixion. "My soul is exceeding sorrowful, even unto death," he says, and in a poignant display of emotion falls to the ground and prays: "O, my Father, if it be possible, let this cup pass from me."

It's an extraordinary and poignant moment—the Son of God confronting the fearful nature of what lies ahead, but the solemn mood is punctured when he returns to the disciples who were keeping watch to find them fast asleep. "Could ye not watch with me one hour?" he says to his embarrassed friends, ". . . the spirit indeed is willing, but the flesh is weak."

Early English writers quickly took up this use of the word "flesh" as shorthand for the worldly, unspiritual part of a person's personality. The flesh was the source of "carnal desires" (from Latin *caro*, meaning "meat") and sinful urges. Chaucer wrote of the "enticings of the flesh" in his *Parson's Tale* (*c.* 1386).

In fact, some medieval holy men were so disgusted with the "weakness" of the flesh that they took to "mortifying" it, starving themselves and flagellating their bodies with whips. Even today, members of the Opus Dei sect of Catholicism wear a spiked chain called a "cilice" for two hours daily in order to injure the flesh and achieve true purity for the spirit.

Take Up the Mantle

[1 Kings 19:19; 2 Kings 2:13]

To take on a role or to inherit someone's authority

This common phrase comes from the story of the prophet Elijah, who picked out his successor—the confusingly named Elisha—by wrapping his mantle or cloak around him. The pair then wander together until the aged Elijah is swept up in a whirlwind and whisked off to heaven. Elisha, we are told, "took up the mantle of Elijah that fell from him" and went off to continue his good works.

Elijah's mantle has been used as a metaphor in English since the seventeenth century. Dryden alluded to the story in 1660 when he wrote in a poem dedicated to fellow poet Sir Robert Howard:

> Yet let me take your mantle up, and I
> Will venture, in your right, to prophesy

Soon, the "prophet" part of the story had dropped out entirely, giving us the familiar usage we know today.

Tender Mercies

....

[Proverbs 12:10; see also e.g. Psalms 25:6 and 40:11]

Used ironically of someone who is unlikely to be either tender or merciful

The Book of Psalms talks a lot about God's "great multitude" of tender mercies, invoking Yahweh's softer side, with varying degrees of hope and desperation. Oddly, though, it is an older and darker use of the phrase that has made the biggest mark on the English language, from the Book of Proverbs: "The tender mercies of the wicked are cruel."

It's a strange expression. Presumably, if the wicked are cruel, they don't have any "tender mercies" at all. In fact,

the phrase could well be based on a mistranslation—
"tender mercies" should be something more like "tender
parts," i.e., innards or guts. Given that the innards were
thought to be the source of human emotion, the proper
meaning of the phrase becomes clear—that wicked people have cruel feelings.

A Thorn in the Flesh

[2 Corinthians 12:7]

A constant irritation

St. Paul, in his Second Letter to the Corinthians, mentions a "thorn in the flesh"—a mysterious ailment sent
"from Satan" to plague him.

But although the expression has become familiar in
English, no one really knows what the original "thorn"
(the word would anyway be better translated as stake, or
fish-hook) actually was. Suggestions have ranged from
earache to epilepsy, from spiritual torment to kidney
stones.

But whatever his affliction, Paul certainly put on a
much braver face than people do today who use the
phrase. The "thorn," he said, was a gift from God "lest I
should be exalted above measure."

Threescore and Ten

[Psalm 90:10]

Seventy years; a lifetime

"Threescore," meaning sixty (a "score" being twenty), is found frequently in the Bible. Most famously, a rather tragic psalm laments the shortness of human life by saying: "The days of our years are threescore years and ten; and if by reason of strength they be fourscore years, yet is their strength labor and sorrow; for it is soon cut off, and we fly away."

As with many biblical phrases, it was Shakespeare who made it famous in the English language, using "threescore and ten" to mean, essentially, a lifetime:

> Threescore and ten I can remember well:
> Within the volume of which time I have seen
> Hours dreadful and things strange
> *Macbeth*, Act 2, Scene 4

Two centuries later, Abraham Lincoln echoed the Book of Psalms when he opened his famous Gettysburg address: "Fourscore and seven years ago . . ." The idea was to achieve a sense of biblical grandeur—and similar motives lie behind most uses of the phrase today.

A Tower of Babel

[Genesis 11:1–9]

**A noisy or confused scene, especially one
where many languages are spoken**

The Book of Genesis tells how humans once attempted to construct a tower that would reach the sky. God prevents this from happening by confusing the languages of the workforce so that suddenly no one can understand each other.

The tower, called Babel by its builders, was never completed but has nonetheless stuck in English as a phrase to describe any chaotic or very multilingual scene. The name itself may be a variant of Babylon (famous for its huge ziggurat temples) or may, as the Bible suggests, be from the verb *balal*, meaning "to confuse." Sadly, as the *Oxford English Dictionary* confirms, the similarity to the English word "babble" is entirely coincidental.

In 1979, the science-fiction writer Douglas Adams alluded to the Genesis story with an imaginary creature called the "babelfish," a small, slug-like animal that could translate any language in the universe and feed telepathic signals directly into a person's brain. The Internet company Yahoo attempted to make this dream a reality with their online translator of the same name. Sadly, the technology to reverse God's curse of mutual unintelligibility has not yet advanced as far as sci-fi authors might have hoped; results produced by automatic translators still range from the incomprehensible to the downright hilarious.

A Tree Shall Be Known by Its Fruit

[Matthew 7:16]

You can tell what a person's like by what they do (not what they say)

In the Sermon on the Mount, Jesus warns his followers against false prophets. But how to tell one from another? Easy, says the Messiah: "Ye shall know them by their fruits. Do men gather grapes of thorns, or figs of thistles?"

The idea, of course, is that if the fruit is bad, the tree must be bad too. It's a nice metaphor, only slightly spoiled by the fact that it's no longer, strictly speaking, true. Modern orchards often grow fruit on special hybrid trees. The top half of an apple tree, for example, is grafted on to the bottom half of a tree from a completely different species. This mutant creation still bears apples as fruit, but the species of the original *tree* is anyone's guess.

Turn One's Face to the Wall

[Isaiah 38:2]

To give up on life

This phrase perfectly captures the essence of despair—that moment when someone turns their back on friends and family at the bedside, and cuts themselves off from the outside world. It comes from the Book of Isaiah, in which King Hezekiah of Judah has just been told he's going to die. Miserably, he "turns his face unto the wall, and prays unto the Lord."

In a marked departure from usual practice, God actually does answer Hezekiah's prayers, giving him a bonus fifteen years of life. But in modern usage, "turning one's face to the wall" rarely implies any hope of divine intervention.

Turn the Other Cheek

[Matthew 5:39; Luke 6:29]

To meekly accept violence; to respond to some insult or injury by inviting more of the same

This instruction, from Jesus' famous Sermon on the Mount, is probably the single clearest statement of the revolutionary Christian morality that distinguished the new religion from the ancient laws of Judaism. "Ye have heard that it hath been said: an eye for an eye, and a tooth for a tooth," Jesus tells his followers. "But I say unto you, that ye resist not evil, but whosoever shall smite thee on thy right cheek, turn to him the other also."

The modern wording has existed since at least 1850, when Oliver Wendell Holmes included it in his poem *Astraea* (it rhymed conveniently with "meek"). In 1913, the early sociologist Gerald Lee neatly described turning the other cheek as "a form of moral jiu-jitsu."

But although you might think the meaning is pretty clear, many believers have, for obvious reasons, found it hard to take the maxim too literally. As conservative commentator Gerard Warner put it, in an article from 2004, "Christians who turn the other cheek don't have a prayer."

A Two-Edged Sword

[Proverbs 5:3–4; Hebrews 4:12; Revelation 1:16]

**Something with dangers as well as benefits;
something that cuts both ways**

The Old Testament Book of Proverbs has the following vivid description of an adulteress's charms: "The lips of a strange woman drop as an honeycomb, and her mouth is smoother than oil. But her end is bitter as wormwood, sharp as a two-edged sword."

In the biblical context, the two-edged sword doesn't mean that there's anything ambiguous about the danger of the "strange woman" (i.e. a woman not linked in marriage). A two-edged sword is simply twice as dangerous as a single-edged sword. "The harlot," as the eighteenth-century theologian John Gill puts it in *An Exposition of the Old Testament* (1762), "hurts both soul and body."

The two-edged sword can also have a positive sense in the Bible. It appears in the Epistle to the Hebrews as a metaphor for the word of God, "piercing even to the dividing asunder of soul and spirit, and of the joints and marrow."

The modern meaning of the phrase emerges in the eighteenth century. As one of the earliest examples (from 1706) has it: "Fame, like a two-edg'd Sword, does cut both ways."

The Wages of Sin

Death—or punishment

St. Paul, in his Letter to the Romans, writes: "The wages of sin is death; but the gift of God is eternal life through Jesus Christ our Lord."

This stern Bible quote has been popular with moralists ever since. Newspaper editorials call for the wages of sin to be paid in full to murderers and drug dealers. Back in 1942, a Milwaukee advice columnist used the phrase to warn girls against illicit trysts with wartime "beaux"—"The price tag for sin," she chided, "has never been changed."

In fact, even murderers have been known to claim their sinner's salary themselves. In one 1987 case, a condemned man from Huntsville, Texas refused to seek a stay of execution because he didn't want to disregard what he saw as a firm biblical instruction.

To Want Someone's Head on a Plate

[Matthew 14:6–11; Mark 6:21–28]

To want someone to be destroyed or punished

This phrase may sound more like a line from a gangster film than a biblical reference, but although the phrasing is modern, the root lies in the Gospels, with the story of St. John the Baptist.

John spent most of his life in the wilderness, preaching about the coming of the Messiah, but in his later years he insulted Herod Antipas, the ruler of Galilee, and ended up in prison. One evening, the story goes, Herod's stepdaughter Salome dances to entertain his guests. Herod is so inflamed by this dance that he promises Salome anything she asks for.

He expects to give her gold or land, but Salome has other, weirder ideas: "Give me," she says, "in a charger [a dish] the head of John the Baptist."

The story was a favorite with artists in the Middle Ages (it offered the perfect combination of sex, death and respectable biblical subject matter), and requesting someone's head on a plate has since become a popular—if rather dramatic—way of wishing a person ill.

To Wash One's Hands of Something

[Matthew 27:24; John 19:1–16]

To disown responsibility; to refuse to bear the blame

After his arrest in the Garden of Gethsemane, Jesus is brought to the Roman governor, Pontius Pilate, to be judged and condemned. It's an extraordinarily dramatic moment in the Bible. On one side are the priests and elders of Jerusalem, calling for Jesus' blood. On the other side is Jesus, bound and silent. Pilate sits in the middle of this burning religious feud, unwilling to execute a clearly innocent man, but also terrified of aggravating the furious mob. "I find no fault in him," says Pilate in John's Gospel, but the crowd return only the relentless refrain: "Crucify [him]! Crucify [him]!"

"When Pilate saw that he could prevail nothing," says Matthew's Gospel, "he took water, and washed his hands before the multitude, saying, I am innocent of the blood of this just person: see ye to it." Jesus is sent to the cross.

This self-exculpatory moment was a favorite with strolling players in the Middle Ages as they re-enacted the Passion of the Christ, and handwashing became a universally recognized metaphor. In his *Macbeth*, Act 5, Scene 1 (published 1623), Shakespeare puts his own dramatic spin on the trope, as Lady Macbeth struggles to cleanse a "damn'd spot" of innocent blood from her murderous hands.

This biblical moment had another, darker, impact too, in the endless medieval discussions of who was to blame for the death of Christ. Pilate says he is "innocent of the blood." The (largely Jewish) crowd reply: "His blood be on us, and on our children"—a curse that has been fuel for anti-Semitic pogroms ever since.

To Be Weighed in the Balance

....

[Daniel 5:27]

To be judged and—usually—found to be deficient

The Book of Daniel tells how that prophet delivered a stern message to King Belshazzar of Babylon: "Thou art weighed in the balances," Daniel tells the king, "and art found wanting."

For us, living in an age of trade standards authorities and labeling laws, the full power of this image is hard to grasp. In ancient economies, however, "balances" or scales were a customer's only defense against the trickery of crooked merchants. The impartiality of the scales could guarantee you were buying the right-sized sack of corn, or the right bag of olives—it was even possible to tell real coins from forged ones because of the different weights of cheap, impure alloys.

Being so central to everyday life, the scales quickly found themselves adopted as metaphors in ancient religion. The Egyptians, for example, believed that the god Osiris weighed the souls of the dead on their way to the afterlife. Those souls that were "found wanting" were thrown to Ammut, the Devourer, a beast with the arms of a lion, the head of a crocodile and the legs of a hippopotamus.

Even today, traditional weighing scales are an international symbol of justice, displayed on statues and coats of arms in law courts across the world.

As White as Snow

[Daniel 7:9; Isaiah 1:18; 2 Kings 5:27]

Very white; (metaphorically) pure or innocent

If you're looking for a simile to prove the point that something really was *very* white, it's hard to get more obvious than snow. The image has been used in English since the Middle Ages, as a symbol of virtue by the *Book of Vices and Virtues* around AD 1200, and as a description of feminine beauty in the *Romance of the Rose*, a century and a half later. Shakespeare uses the phrase in *Hamlet*, Act 3, Scene 3 (1602) as a metaphor for innocence—as we still do today with the expression "whiter than white."

In 1611, the appearance of the King James Bible gave the phrase new authority by showing that it went back even to the days of the ancient prophets. Sometimes, as in the Book of Daniel, it is a stock description of God's shining garments. In Isaiah, it describes the purification of sins. In Kings, however, it has a darker meaning: to be "white as snow" is to be a leper—because the disease turns the skin of its victims dead and white.

It might seem strange to find mentions of frozen water in a book from the hot lands of the Middle East—but biblical authors did have experience of snow. Winters were often surprisingly cold in Israel, and even in summer you can usually find snow on the peaks of the Lebanon range. In fact, this snow was sometimes imported to the lowlands as a primitive form of refrigeration.

The Wisdom of Solomon

[1 Kings 4:31]

Great wisdom or discernment

After David, Solomon is the most famous of the Bible's great Israelite kings. Legendary for his wealth, he was the last king to rule over both Israel and Judah and is credited with building the first temple in Jerusalem. As a cultural figure he casts a long shadow, inspiring everyone from Islamic scholars (who revere him as the prophet Sulaiman, controller of winds and master of jinn) to Victorian adventure stories like H. Rider Haggard's *King Solomon's Mines* (1885).

More than anything, though, Solomon is remembered as the proverbial embodiment of human wisdom. "He was wiser than all men," says the First Book of Kings, "and his fame was in all nations round about." Among his admirers was the great Queen of Sheba (thought to be in modern-day Yemen), who was so impressed by his mind that she traveled all the way from her kingdom with four and a half tons of gold by way of hello.

The Sheban Queen wasn't the last woman to have been swept off her feet by the combination of intellect and political power. The French first lady, Carla Bruni, boasted in 2008 of how her husband, President Sarkozy, appeared to have "five or even six brains."

The Judgment of Solomon

Solomon's most famous moment of wisdom came when he judged a case between two women who lived in the same house and who had given birth at the same time. One woman's child had died. Then, it was alleged, she had stolen the other woman's living one, claiming it as her own and leaving the dead child in its place.

Easy! said Solomon. He called for a sword and made as if to cut the living baby in two. His plan? If two women claim the same baby, "give half to the one, and half to the other."

This produced dramatic but opposite reactions. The false mother stood by, content that if she couldn't have a live baby, at least no one would. The real mother, by contrast, immediately gave up her claim on the child, preferring to give it away than to watch it die. So the truth was revealed, and the real mother took her baby home.

A Wolf in Sheep's Clothing

[Matthew 7:15]

A person with evil intent who tries to make himself appear harmless

"Beware of false prophets," says Jesus in the Sermon on the Mount. They "come to you in sheep's clothing, but inwardly they are ravening wolves."

It sounds like an odd image, but so-called "aggressive mimicry" is often found in nature. Female bolas spiders, for example, can mimic the scent of moths, in order to attract other moths into their clutches. Baby cuckoos in other birds' nests imitate their adopted siblings before finally killing them.

That said, a wolf that dressed up in sheep's clothing could be accused of making a bit of a strategic blunder, as an old fairy tale (by the twelfth-century Greek author Nikephoros Basilakis) shows. The wolf in this story lives the high life for a bit, dining out on the unwitting sheep that surround him. He soon meets his end, however, when the shepherd decides he fancies a nice bit of mutton.

The Writing's on the Wall

[Daniel 5]

The game's up; disaster is imminent

The Book of Daniel tells of a strange vision seen by King Belshazzar of Babylon. The king is feasting when, suddenly, a ghostly hand appears and writes four mysterious words upon the wall: "mene, mene, tekel, upharsin."

Belshazzar summons the prophet Daniel to interpret the apparition, and the news is bad. "God," says Daniel, "hath numbered thy kingdom, and finished it." That very night, Belshazzar is killed and his kingdom taken over by the Persians.

Although the story has always been well known and popular, the modern wording of the phrase appears first in a poem by Swift from around 1720, which, by chance, remains remarkably relevant today:

> A baited Banker thus desponds,
> From his own Hand foresees his Fall;
> They have his Soul who have his Bonds;
> 'Tis like the Writing on the Wall.

Ye of Little Faith

[Matthew 6:30, 8:26, 16:18; Luke 12:28]

You doubters! (often said when one has just proved doubters wrong)

Jesus wasn't well-known for being a tease, but it's hard not to see a flicker of humor in the way he constantly reproaches his disciples when he's about to do something miraculous.

The Gospel of Matthew tells of a time when his unfortunate followers were caught in a storm on the Sea of Galilee. "Lord, save us: we perish," cried the terrified crew, quite reasonably. "Why are ye fearful, O ye of little faith?" is Jesus' reply. "Then he arose, and rebuked the winds and the sea; and there was a great calm."

Seventeenth-century commentators, anxious to defend the holy apostles, dutifully pointed out that at least Jesus credited his followers with *some* faith. They were, therefore, "petty fidians" as opposed to being dreaded "nullfidians"—those with no faith at all.

But, in modern speech at least, "ye of little faith" is rarely a very serious rebuke. One California newspaper, for example, used the phrase in 2004 to describe Americans who were refusing to support the USA Olympic Basketball Team.

You Cannot Serve God and Mammon

[Matthew 6:24]

It's impossible to seek worldly wealth and spiritual salvation at the same time

Of all the many devils of Christianity—Beelzebub, Leviathan, Asmodeus, Appolyon and the rest—Mammon, the spirit of wealth and greed, is perhaps the best known today. He probably owes his modern notoriety to the famous excesses of Wall Street brokers and "City boys" back in the eighties, and even more to the perceived role of bankers in the financial crisis of 2008.

In the New Testament, "mammon" simply means "wealth" (from the Aramaic *māmoˉnā*). When Jesus says "ye cannot serve God and Mammon," in Matthew's Gospel, it's a straightforward statement about material riches, not a cosmic clash between rival deities. However, the old human tendency to personify abstract ideas—along with some iffy translating—quickly turned this perfectly ordinary word into Mammon, one of the great demonic princes of the underworld. William Langland gives him an early mention in *Piers Plowman* (c.1390), but he really comes alive as a character in Edmund Spenser's great Elizabethan epic *The Faerie Queene,* where he is characterized as "an uncouth, savage and uncivil wight" with sooty hands and "nails like claws."

In 1667, with Milton's *Paradise Lost*, the picture gets even less flattering. Mammon, says the poet, has a hunched back because while in Heaven he couldn't stop bending over to ogle the golden floors. Perhaps Ambrose Bierce puts it best, though, in his *Devil's Dictionary* of 1906: "Mammon, n.—The god of the world's leading religion. The chief temple is in the holy city of New York."

Bibliography

Barnes, Albert, *Notes on the New Testament* (1868)

Crystal, David, *Begat: The King James Bible and the English Language* (2010)

Delitzsch, Franz; Keil, Carl Friedrich, *Biblical Commentary on the Old Testament* (1857)

Easton, Matthew George, *Easton's Bible Dictionary* (1897)

Gill, John, *An Exposition of the New Testament* (1746)

Gill, John, *An Exposition of the Old Testament* (1762)

Hendrickson, Robert, *Encyclopaedia of Word and Phrase Origins* (4th Edition 2008)

Room, Adrian (Ed.) *Brewers Dictionary of Phrase and Fable* (16th Edition, 1999)

The Oxford English Dictionary (OED Online Edition)

Speake, Jennifer (Ed.) *Oxford Dictionary of Proverbs* (2008)

Vincent, Marvin R., *Word Studies in the New Testament* (1887)

Index

....

A

Aaron, 62, 63, 105
Abel, 10–11, 84
Abraham, 105–106, 130
abundance, 23
Adam, 1, 11, 16, 40, 46, 49, 65, 124
Adam's Apple, 1–2
Adams, Douglas, 139
adrenalin, 67
adulteresses, 143
age, 103
agricultural produce, best, 42
Alfred, King, 4
amen, use of, 2
Amen corner, 3
Amen to That, 2–3
Americans, 76
Anaximenes, 18
anger, 87–88, 131
"Another One Bites the Dust"
    (song), 16
apocalypse, 127
Apocryphal Story, An, 3–4
Apple of My Eye, The, 4–5
Apres Moi le Déluge, 5–6
As Old as Methuselah, 103
As White as Snow, 148–149
Asimov, Isaac, 89
Astracea (poem), 142
Atwood, Margaret, 7
authorities, 108–109
avarice, 118, 126

B

Baal, 75
Babylon, 31, 56, 73, 139

balm, 6–7
Baptism of Fire, A, 7–8
baptisms, 8
Basilakis, Nikephoros, 152
Be All Things to All Men, 8–9
Beam in Your Own Eye, The,
    9–10
Bear the Mark of Cain, 10–11
behemoth, A, 14
Belshazzar, King, 147, 153
Bible, 113
Bible (King James), viii–x, 88
    Acts, 15, 24, 50, 55, 77, 79,
        98,120
    2 Chronicles, 78
    1 Corinthians, 8, 111, 137
    Daniel, 43, 89, 147, 153
    Deuteronomy, 2, 3, 4, 33, 51,
        94, 117
    Ecclesiastes, 32, 36, 65, 92, 102
    Ephesians, 87
    Ezekiel, 47, 125
    Exodus, 37, 48, 62, 72, 97
    Galatians, 40, 93, 115, 126
    Genesis, 1, 5, 10, 16, 18, 40, 42,
        46, 47, 49, 50, 84, 88, 103,
        105, 106, 123, 129, 133, 139
    Hebrews, 82, 143
    Hosea, 114
    Isaiah, 13, 17, 31, 32, 47, 68, 83,
        95, 101, 112, 124, 141, 148
    James, 64
    Jeremiah, 6, 73, 83, 85, 125
    Job, 14, 16, 33, 35, 55, 64, 103
    John, 22, 30, 77, 83, 86, 122, 146
    Joshua, 57

Jude, 129
Judges, 38, 106
1 Kings, 57, 74, 75, 78, 135, 149
2 Kings, 53, 75, 135, 148
Lamentations, 73
Leviticus, 93, 105, 121
Luke, 21, 22, 28, 29, 50, 52, 59,
    60, 77, 100, 107, 110, 142,
    154
Mark, 22, 41, 53, 54, 55, 77,
    126, 145
Mathew, 2, 3, 7, 9, 17, 19, 21,
    22, 28, 34, 41, 54, 67, 69, 77,
    80, 81, 91, 93, 94, 99, 104,
    116–117, 117, 119, 122, 127,
    128, 132, 134, 140, 142, 145,
    146, 152, 154, 155
Micah, 16
1 Peter, 20, 53
Proverbs, 96, 126, 131, 136, 143
Psalms, 4–5, 16, 23, 47, 56, 61,
    104, 136, 138
Revelation, 47, 61, 98, 143
Romans, 66, 108, 144
Samuel, 70
1 Samuel, 12, 25, 27–28
2 Samuel, 27, 58, 76
1 Timothy, 45, 118
1 Thessalonians, 82
Zechariah, 33
Bibliotheca Politica, 109
Bierce, Ambrose, 156
Bite the Dust, 16
Blind Leading the Blind, The,
    17–18
Book of Vices and Virtues, 148
Borges, Jorge Luis, 77
Breathe Life into Something,
    18–19
Bruegel Pieter, the Elder, 17
Bryon, Lord, 44
Bullen, Frank T., 51
Burns, Robert, 96

Butler, Samuel, 57
Byrds, The (musical group), 36

C

Cain, vii, 10–11, 84
Calment, Jeanne, 103
Cast Pearls Before Swine, 19–20
Chaucer, Geoffrey, 84, 123, 135
Christianity, dying for, 98, 128
Christie, Agatha, 2
Churchill, Winston, ix
Cohen, Leonard, 62
Coleridge, Samuel Taylor, ix
Collins, Margaret, 80
Collins, Tim, 10
conversions, sudden, 24–25
Cooke, Alistair, 89
Coventry Carol, 128
Cover a Multitude of Sins, 20
Cross to Bear, A, 21
crucifixion, 21, 22, 30, 53, 134,
    146
cruelty, 136–137
Cruise of the Cachalot (Bullen), 51
Cupid's Revenge (play), 72

D

Dahl, Roald, 51, 84
Damascene Conversion, A, 24–25
damnation, threat of, 47
Daniel, 44, 89-90, 147, 153
Dante, 77, 88, 118, 126
David, King, 12, 26, 27–28, 58,
    71, 107
David and Goliath Contest, A,
    25–26
David and Jonathan, 27–28
Dawkins, Richard, ix, 118–119
Day of Atonement, 121
Dekker, Thomas, 57
Delilah, 39
Dickens, Charles, 19
dignity, men's, 12

dinosaur ants, 81
disaster, 80–81, 153
Disciple, A, 28
disciples, 28, 119
Do As You Would Be
    Done By, 29
Dombey and Son (Dickens), 19
doubters, 30, 154
Doubting Thomas, A, 30
Drop in the Bucket, A, 31
Dryden, John, 136
dust, 16

E

earth, shape of, 33
Eat, Drink and Be Merry, 32
Egypt and Egyptians, 62–64
Elijah, 135
Elisha, 135
End of the Earth, The, 33
Epiphany, An, 34
Escape by the Skin of One's Teeth,
    35
Eve, 40, 46, 49, 123
evil, problem of, 65
evil eye, 54
evil intent, 152
executions, 21, 22
existence, of mankind, 49
Exposition of the Old Testament, An
    (Gill), 143
Eye for an Eye, An, 37
Eyeless in Gaza, 38
eyes, 4–5

F

Faerie Queen, The (Spenser), 155
Fall from Grace, 40
Fall on Stony Ground, 41
fasting, 94
Fat of the Land, The, 42
favor, fallen from, 40
Feast of Epiphany, 34

Feet of Clay, 43–44
Fig Leaf, A, 46
Fight the Good Fight, 45
Fincher, David, 126
Fire and Brimstone, 47
Fire and Brimstone in Hell
    (Thomas), 47
flat-earthers, 33
flesh, mortification of, 135
Fleshpot, A, 48
football, 60
Forbidden Fruit, 49
Fox, George, 29, 113
Fruit of One's Loins, The, 50

G

Galatians, 40
Gall and Wormwood, 51
Garden of Eden, expulsion from,
    40, 49
Gaza Strip, 38
Get Thee Behind Me, Satan,
    52–53
Gettysburg address, 138
Gilead, 6–7
Gill, John, 102, 143
gird, 53
Give Someone the Evil Eye, 54
Give Up the Ghost, 55
Go from Strength to Strength, 56
Go the Way of All Flesh, 57
Go to Jericho, 58
goats, 122
God, 47, 72, 73, 74, 77–78, 85,
    136, 155
godsends, 97
Golden Rule, 29
Goliath, 12, 26, 27
good causes, working for, 45
Good Samaritan, A, 59–60
Gray, Thomas, 66
Gulliver's Travels (Swift), 85

H

Hail Mary (*Ave Maria*), 60–61
Hail Mary Pass, A, 60–61
Hamlet (play), 132, 148–149
Hammet, Samuel, 79
Handmaiden's Tale, The (Atwood), 7
Hanun, King, 58
Hardy, Lois Hunt, 81
Hardy, Thomas, 71
Harper's Magazine, 101
Harris, Arthur "Bomber," 114
Harvey, Gabriel, 14
He Who Increases Knowledge Increases Sorrow, 65–66
Heart's Desire, The, 66
Henry IV Part 1 (play), 125
Henry IV Part 2 (play), 98
Herod, King, 128
Herod Agrippa, King, 55
Herod Antipas, 145
hexes, 54
Hezekiah, King, 124, 141
Hitchens, Christopher, ix
Holier Than Thou, 68–69
Holmes, Oliver Wendell, 142
Holy Innocents, 128
Hosea, 114
House Divided Against Itself Cannot Stand, A, 69–70
How the Mighty Have Fallen, 70–71
Howard, Robert, 136
Huxley, Aldous, 38

I

I Am What I Am, 72
infanticide, 126
Inferno (Dante), 88, 118, 126
innocence, 40, 83–84, 148–149
Isaac, sacrifice of, 105–106
Israelites, 62–64, 97, 105, 114

It's Better to Give than to Receive, 15
Ivanhoe (Scott), 85

J

Jacob, 5
James I, King, viii
Jehoshaphat, 78–79
Jeremiad, A, 73–74
Jeremiah, 73, 85
Jericho, 58, 59
Jeroboam, A, 74
Jeroboam, King, 74
Jesus, 9, 15, 17, 37, 41, 49, 52, 54, 55, 68, 69, 77, 91, 95, 99, 104, 107–108, 116, 117–118, 122, 134
  birth of, 100
  blame for death, 147
  central commandments, 93
  fasting, 94
  miracles of, 154
  prophecies about, 83, 95
  teachings of, 142
Jezebel, 75
Jezebel, A, 75–76
Job, 64–65
John the Baptist, 8, 99, 145
Jonathan, 27–28, 71
Jonathan, A, 76
Joseph, 42
Joshua, 59
Journal of Abnormal Psychology, 66
Judah, 73
Judaism, 142, 147
Judas, A, 77
Judas Iscariot, 28, 77–78, 80
judgments, 147–148
Jumping Jehoshaphat, 78–79
justice, symbol of, 148

K

Kick Against the Pricks, 79–80
King Leir (play), 2
Kipling, Rudyard, 109
Kiss of Death, 80–81
Kiss of Life, 81–82
knowledge, 65–66
Knox, John, 75

L

Labor of Love, A, 82
Lamb to the Slaughter, 83–84
"Lamb to the Slaughter, A" (Dahl), 84
Land of Nod, The, 84–85
Langland, William, 10, 19
larynx, 1
Lee, Gerald, 142
Leeson, Jane, 132
Leopard Can't Change His Spots, A, 85–86
leopards, 86
lepers, 149
Let He Who Is Without Sin Cast the First Stone, 86–87
Let Not the Sun Go Down on Your Wrath, 87–88
Let There Be Light, 88
Lincoln, Abraham, 70, 95, 138
Lion's Den, A, 89–90
Little Britain (TV show), 54
Little Orphan Annie (cartoon), 101
Live by the Sword, Die by the Sword, 91–92
Living Dog Is Better than a Dead Lion, A, 92
loins, 50, 53
Lot, 130
Louis Napoleon, Prince, 7
Love Thy Neighbor, 92
Love's Labor Lost (play), 83
Lowell, James, 76

M

Macbeth (play), 146–147
Mad Men (TV show), 115
Madame de Pompadour, 5
Mafia, 80
Magi, 34
malice, 54
Mammon, 155–156
Man Does Not Live by Bread Alone, 94
Man of Law's Tale (Chaucer), 84
Man of Sorrows, A, 95
Man Proposes but God Disposes, 96
manna, 97
Manna from Heaven, 97
Marmion (Scott), 12
Martyr, A, 98–99
massacres, 126
masturbation, 133–134
Matsell, G. W., 129
Megadeath (musical group), 35
Metallica (musical group), 69
Methuselah, 103
Milton, John, 38, 62, 156
misrepresentation, 112
modesty, 46
money, 118–119
Monsell, John, 45
Moore, Thomas, 92
morality, Christian, 142
Morbus pedicularis, 55
Mormon Church, 10
Morris, Gouverneur, 91
Moses, 62, 94
Motion, Andrew, x
Munro, Neil, 120
murderers, guilt of, 10–11
Mustaine, Dave, 35
My Cup Runneth Over, 23
Mysterious Affair at Styles, The (Christie), 2

N

Napoleon, 44
Nashe, Thomas, 14
Nazareth, 107–108
Nebuchadnezzar, King, 43–44
Nest of Vipers, A, 99
New Statesman, 129
No Balm in Gilead, 6–7
No Rest for the Wicked, 101
No Room at the Inn, 100
Nothing New Under the Sun, 102
nudity, 46

O

Obama, Barack, 111
Ode to Napoleon (Byron), 44
Onan, 133, 134
Onania, 133–134
organization, of self, 124
Out of the Mouths of Babes, 104

P

parables, 9, 41, 59
Paradise Lost (Milton), 62, 156
Parker, Dorothy, 19–20
Parson's Tale (Chaucer), 135
Paul the Apostle, 24–25
peace, 13
Peace Offering, A, 105
people
    chameleon-like, 8–9
    evil/wicked, 99, 101
    uncultured, 106–107
    virtuous, 119
Pharisees, 69, 77, 86
Philistine, A, 106–107
Philistines, 106–107
Physician, Heal Thyself, 107–108
Picture of Dorian Gray, The
    (Wilde)
Piers Plowman (Langland), 10, 19
piety, 68
plagues, Egyptian, 63

Pollard, Vicky, 54
Pontius Pilate, 146
popes, infallibility of, 112
power and powerlessness, 38,
    70–71
Powers That Be, The, 108–109
Prodigal Son, A, 110–111
prostitutes, 75
proverbs, 65, 79, 96, 116, 125
Psalm 23, 24
pupils (eyes), 4–5
purity, 40, 86–87, 148–149
Put Away Childish Things, 111
Put Words in Someone's Mouth,
    112
Pythagoras, 87

Q

qi, 19–20
Queen (musical group), 16
Quote Chapter and Verse, 113

R

Reap the Whirlwind, 114
rebellion, 79–80
reconciliation, 87–88, 105
Red Sky at Night, Shepherd's
    Delight, Red Sky in Morning,
    Shepherd's Warning, 116–117
Reed, Lou, 115
reinvigoration, 18–19, 81
relationships, homosexual, 27–28,
    129–130
responses, 131
responsibility, disowning of, 146
resuscitation, 81–82
retribution, 37
Richard III (play), 77
rocks, 117
Rockwell, Lew, 100
Rogue's Lexicon (Matsell), 129
Romance of the Rose, 148
Roosevelt, Theodore, 131

Root of All Evil, The, 118–119
Russell, John, 107

S

sacrifices, 105–106
Salome, 145
Salt of the Earth, The, 119–120
Sam Slick in Texas (Hammet), 79
Samaritans, 60
Samson, 38, 39
Samson Agonistes (Milton), 38
Samson and Delilah, 39
Satan, 124
sayings, Wild West, 16, 79
scales, 147–148
Scapegoat, A, 121
Science (magazine), 15
Scott, Walter, 12, 62, 85
Seeger, Pete, 36
Sentamu, John, 100
Separate the Sheep from the
    Goats, 122
Sermon on the Mount, 9, 37, 132,
    140, 142, 152
sermons, terrifying, 47
Set One's House in Order, 124
Set Someone's Teeth on Edge, 125
Seven (movie), 126
Seven Deadly Sins, 126
Shakespeare, William, 77, 83,
    98, 116, 123, 125, 132, 138,
    146–147, 148
sheep, 122
Shenton, Daniel, 33
Sign of the Times, A, 127
Sin of Onan, The, 133–134
Sins, 101, 121, 126
situations, dangerous, 89–90
skies, red, 117–118
skin, black, 11
Slaughter of the Innocents, A,
    128–129
Slaughter of the Innocents (movie),

128–129
slaves and slavery, 11, 70
snakes, 99, 123–124
Sod, 129–130
Sod's Law, 129–130
Sodom and Sodomites, 129, 130
Soft Answers Turn Away Wrath,
    A, 131
Solomon, King, 66, 131, 149–151
    judgment of, 151
Spenser, Edmund, 155
Spirit Is Willing, but the Flesh Is
    Weak, The, 134–135
St. Paul, 8–9, 15, 40, 45, 66, 79,
    82, 87, 91, 93, 108, 111, 115,
    118, 137, 144
    conversion of, 120
St. Peter, 52–53, 117–118
St. Stephen, 98
St. Thomas, 30
Staubach, Roger, 61
Straight and Narrow, The,
    132–133
strength, through unity, 69–70
suffering, 64, 65, 95, 98
sulfur, 47
Summoner's Tale (Chaucer), 123
Swift, Jonathan, 84, 153

T

Take Up the Mantle, 135–136
talents, concealed/wasted, 67–68
Tales of My Landlord (Scott), 62
Temptation of Christ, 52
temptations, 49, 52
Tender Mercies, 136–137
Tess of the D'Urbervilles (Hardy),
    71
There's a Serpent in Every
    Paradise, 123–124
Thessalonica, 82
Thomas à Kempis, 96
Thorn in the Flesh, 137–138

Threescore and Ten, 138
To a Mouse (poem), 96
To Be Someone's Rock, 117–118
To Be Weighed in the Balance, 147–148
To Beard the Lion, 12
To Beat Swords into Plowshares, 13–14
To Crucify, 22
To Everything There is a Season, 36
To Gird One's Loins, 53
To Harden One's Own Heart, 62–64
To Have the Patience of Job, 64–65
To Have the Scales Fall from One's Eyes, 120
To Hide One's Talent Under a Bushel, 67
To Want Someone's Head on a Plate, 145
To Wash One's Hands of Something, 146–147
torment, 22, 101
Tower of Babel, A, 139–140
traitors, 77, 99
Tree Shall be Known by Its Fruit, A, 140
Trumbull, Jonathan, 76
"Turn! Turn! Turn!" (song), 36
Turn One's Face to the Wall, 141
Turn the Other Cheek, 142
Two-Edged Sword, A, 143
Tyndale, William, viii
Tyrrell, James, 109

V

Vedas, Hindu, 18
Venus and Adonis (poem), 116
verses, Bible, 113

Vincent, Thomas, 47
violence, 91, 142
virility, 12
virtuousness, 68, 132–133, 148

W

Wages of Sin, The, 144
wanderers, 110–111
war, end of, 13
Warner, Gerard, 142
Washington, George, 76
wealth, 155
weapons, 13
weather forecasting, 116–117
Webster, John, 57
Westward Ho! (Webster and Dekker), 57
Weyman, Stanley, 92
Wilde, Oscar, 72
wine bottles, 74, 103
wisdom, 104, 149–150
Wisdom of Solomon, The, 149–150
Wolf in Sheep's Clothing, A, 152
women, wicked, 75
Woodforde, James, 58
words, God's, 112
world, creation of, 88–89
wormwood, 51
Writing's on the Wall, 153
Wycliffe, John, viii, 2

Y

Ye of Little Faith, 154
You Cannot Serve God and Mammon, 155–156
You Reap What You Sow, 115

Also Available from Reader's Digest

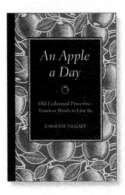